Spiritual Revolution

Unconventional Life Lessons from My Teachers

www.vrajdevi.com

ISBN: 979-8-3602-3831-7

Cover design
Mary Ellen Sanger

Dedication

THIS BOOK MANIFESTS FROM A few old journals that I kept from over the years in which I wrote during my travels around this beautiful planet. The narrative draws from my personal experiences, interspersed with inspirational characters from my life. When I first started transcribing these stories from paper onto the computer, I thought that I would share them only as private memoirs for my son and any future generations.

Although when I started writing, more stories poured out like an unstoppable torrent. I understood that these stories needed to be shared beyond my home comfort zone. By sharing some of my profound personal experiences and truth, I hope that you may connect to your own story, truth and ultimate healing.

I feel blessed to have met many exceptional teachers and friends along the path of life; some teachers I spent many years with and some only momentarily, in the most unexpected places, and of all ages, and walks of life. It is said that even a single moment spent with a great soul can transform your life – when the student is ready the teacher will and *does* appear.

I dedicate this book to all the lives within these pages, and to all the other dear souls who have touched my life and heart. You know who you are. Over and over again I bow in honour, love, and respect to you. We are forever connected. Thank you.

I also dedicate this book to you, the reader. You are meant to have found this book. What a unique gift you are. Thank you for dedicating your time to read this book, an offering that may encourage and inspire you along this journey of the heart with all the many waves of love life brings.

> *Life's waves can hit with such force, knock you down so hard that you may feel it impossible to get up again. Then there are other waves that you will ride with ease and grace, floating in an ocean of infinite love. Whichever wave you may be riding right now, know that you are only one breath away from change if you desire. There is no limit to the power of the human spirit – your spirit.*

You may have heard recently `*there are great shifts happening right now.*´ There always has and always will be great transformation available to you or me or anyone. The time really is only now. We are here to support one another on this journey of life; however one must act and do the inner work for oneself. No one can give that to you, we can guide and assist each other, but the daily effort must come from within oneself. There is a Spiritual revolution happening right now and you are a part of it.

Eternally I bow, honour and salute you; you are the ones we have been waiting for.

With love Vrajdevi

> *"Loving ourselves through the process of owning our story is the bravest thing we will ever do."*

- Brene Brown

I WAS IN NEW YORK city staying with a friend. Just days before leaving for my long-awaited ashram experience in India, I received an urgent email from a friend in New Zealand. I rushed to open it, my heart pounding.

The subject read "*Urgent: Please call home.*"

It didn't make sense. I had nothing urgent happening with this old high school friend I hadn't seen in years.

I clicked to open. "*Your sister is missing. Your family is trying to contact you. You must go home immediately.*"

My heart sank, and I read the email again, my thoughts a sudden tsunami of panic. I raced to use the phone in the apartment to call home. The messages on the voicemail were full. I tried again and again and again. Finally, my mother picked up, wailing. I could barely understand her words. My sister was *gone.*

Understanding little, I knew that I had to get on the next flight home to New Zealand. I cancelled my India trip and planned to leave on the first plane out. That night I could not sleep, I could not stop thinking, wondering, *is my sister, OK*? I know she is fine, yes everything will be fine. Calm down, everything will be alright.

Then my dream resurfaced. Months ago, during a trip to Egypt, I dreamt that my mother called, distressed because my sister was… *missing.* She was crying, I was crying. I woke up that night with a start, sweating, crying, moaning in deep emotional pain. My heart was on fire, a razor-sharp arrow lodged deep inside. I pulled out my sister's picture that I carried with me everywhere and apologised to her for the senseless dream. I meditated to shake off that horror and banished the dream.

Now, anxious to be on the flight home, I pulled out that same dear photo, and placed her in front of me, meditating again for calm.

"Where are you honey?"

"I am right here," she said.

"Right here? No, no you are not. You are somewhere in New Zealand. I am coming home to find you. Tell me exactly where you are now."

The same answer kept coming again and again.

I'm here.

Back in New Zealand, for days after my sister's disappearance, a thick white mist engulfed the land along the west coast, like a floating fluffy blanket of snow. Driving through the mist, my family and I were unable to see more than a few metres ahead of the car.

The local people would later tell me how they had never seen such a thick mist there in Piha, and never for so long, for so many days.

Goddess *Hinepukohurangi*[1]. Her mist places delicate touches throughout the land. She is integral to the very life breath of the land and people. She is spellbinding.

Had *Hinepukohurangi* come to take my sister by the hand, to take her child-of-the-mist home with her? I could not shake her unusual and insistent presence, afraid of what it could mean. Deep in my gut I felt a twisted pain. I needed answers.

"What have you done? Answer me. Where is she? Where is my sister? What have you done?"

I ran to the ocean scolding, furious, confused, and in utter despair.

I learned from the police on the scene that in the early hours of October 11th, 2004, my sister made a call to their emergency line. Everything went so wrong after that.

1 See endnotes.

Māori roots and early life in New Zealand

As a child, I spent sunlit hours in the garden with my sisters. I am third in a line of four girls. One adventurous day, three of us climbed up the tallest pine tree in our front garden. I encouraged my sisters to keep climbing while I spirited ahead unafraid, my hair yanked by the leaves, twigs and branches now a tangle upon my brown locks.

"Come on. It's amazing up here. You guys are missing out." I grinned, trying to persuade my sisters, still only halfway up.

I was always the instigator, the eager one excited to muster up as much mischief as possible. The eldest sister was not around most of the time. She was the cool one, with ten years between her and our youngest sister. The second sister was the sensitive and sneaky one. By the time my parents had their fourth daughter, they spoiled her some, making up for the mistakes they had made with the first three of us.

My two sisters finally made it to the top, complaining all the way. We looked beyond our house into the horizon. A sea of roofs and trees flowed over the rolling hills, and we perched like little Tui birds in our own secret sunny tree. We fluffed our wings and held tight to our branches.

The sun dipped in the sky and the peace we found at the top of the tree made time stand still. Suspended in bliss, we snuggled up to each other, safe in our new bird's nest home.

Until Mother screamed.

"Where are you, kids?" That anxious tone was all too familiar to us.

She rushed around trying to find us, ever more frantic. She'd never spot us in our secret nest, we thought, and tried to hold back our laughter as she skittered about like a nervous bird mama. When we could hold back no longer, we erupted in a roar of giggles.

"What are you doing up there? It's dangerous! Get down NOW." Mother screamed with more intensity. We were laughing so hard we couldn't respond.

Our mother was so beautiful as a young woman. Her family came to New Zealand as settlers from Scotland, and she reflected the breath-taking natural beauty of the highlands. It is no wonder the handsome young men of her small back-country town fawned over her. When she became pregnant at the age of 19, her parents were furious. The father was a local Māori boy who, despite pounding threats from my mother's father, never accepted the child or came forth with support.

Enduring the judgments of her rural town as a young, unwed mother, and the disdain from her own parents, my mother jumped at an invitation to move in with friends in Australia. She was ready to fly away, and off she went on wishful wings, with my eldest sister in tow, a toddler of just two or three. Mother had no idea there was a plan afoot.

The plan, hatched by the sister of the Māori boy, father of my mother's child, was to introduce my mother to *another* brother. Kind, quiet, and shy, my mother's beauty opened doors, and in walked my father. My second sister was born in Sydney. In another two years I was born in Melbourne. My mother's young, growing family was not joyous. Life with my father was centred around crazy parties, crazy nights, and crazy explosive abuse. Too much crazy for the country girl, and my mother planned her escape back to New Zealand.

With her three girls, she bravely flew from my father and the emotional violence of those days. Hard as it was to bear her mother's scorn, it was easier to bear than her husband's outbursts. Familial and societal pressure would eventually force them back together, and the desperate confusion, insecurity, and anxiety of those times came to define her, accompanying all our days as we grew.

Back in our bird's nest, we watched her anxiety grow. It would become much clearer as we grew older, that the anxiety our mother experienced throughout her young life, contributed to her low self-worth, and her constant worry about being safe and settled.

We knew she would not climb to force us down, so we decided to enjoy our peace, remaining a little longer in the final rays of a setting sun. Glowing orange and red turned to purple and deep blue, our hearts full of the wonder around us, far away from the explosive home below. In that swift yet infinite moment, we were blissful, fully content.

I led my sisters into a heartfelt rendition of the popular Carpenters song *"Top of the world."* It was fitting, buzzing, I couldn't keep the song inside. Joy always spilled out into the world through songs for me.

> *"I'm on the top of the world looking down on creation and the only explanation I can find. Is the love that I found ever since you've been around. Your love puts me on the top of the world."*

Then Father's car approached.

In a flash, we scrambled down the tree, hearts racing. The magic sunset went suddenly dark, and we scurried inside to the dinner table. Mother was clearly annoyed. Father entered, as usual, swearing. Heavy dark clouds entered with him, engulfing us in a black hole with no clear exit.

We knew all too well that at any moment this man could turn into a demon from the underworld, firing dragon-like fury upon us. Sometimes this fury was so great that his arms would turn into weapons, towards Mother, towards us. We sat still and quiet, chewing our broccoli without making a peep.

Our father came from a dysfunctional family: physical, verbal, and emotional abuse was the stuff of everyday life. His mother was violent and unstable. His father was the local playboy. Their seven children suffered without role models, without direction. My father left home when he was 17 years old, to pursue a career in custom automotive painting, eventually landing in Australia, where, no longer bound to his abusive family past, he achieved a sense of freedom and space that he had never experienced before.

That changed when he met our mother. He never quite accepted her firstborn child, resenting that she was his younger brother's child. He hated providing for her, but also for us. He never got the boy he wanted, 'just girls.' That my mother was not able to give him a son was a defect in his eyes.

Night after night: Father screaming, firing his dragon fury over Mother. The pattern of violence he had learned in his home as a child, carried into our lives, gripped our entire household. My sisters and I held each other tight, fearing the worst. How we wanted to help, but how small and helpless we were, in our bedroom trembling. For hours and hours, the demon's fury raged, and we cried ourselves to sleep, under our bed covers, far as we could get from the madness, praying that the storm would pass.

Modern-day Māori men and women come from great lineages of fierce warriors. Some of my genetics are from these Polynesian warriors and healers of power and prestige, who traversed the great Pacific *Moananui-a-kiwa* numerous times. In history classes in school, we learned about the atrocities of Hitler in Nazi Germany or the apartheid oppression of Black people in South Africa, our own New Zealand history overshadowed. I had to learn about our history many years later in my early twenties, through a journey of self-discovery.

I discovered stories about empowered women including Muriwai and Wairaka, my direct ancestors. Muriwai was the sister of Toroa, the captain of the famous *Mataatua waka*[2]. She was a powerful woman and *Tohunga*[3] who lived over six centuries ago. Wairaka was the daughter of Toroa the captain of the *waka*. They came from Hawaii, with other tribal members arriving in New Zealand near my current day tribal lands of Bay of Plenty.

There are many magical stories about how these women lived. It is important to recognise that in our ancient Polynesian traditions, women held positions of high esteem in society, equal to men in terms of everyday life. Women could be warriors, landowners, teachers and healers.

It was not until the British arrived in New Zealand as the first non-Polynesians, that the idea of putting women below men was implanted into the consciousness of the Māori men. Before British thought seeped into New Zealand, women and men were honoured as equals within Māori society.

Today, we have a better framework for this disempowerment of the feminine; defying the age-old belief that women are limited, demonstrating what we know today as women's empowerment. My encounter with these stories and my direct connection to them marked the beginning of my self-discovery journey and toward recognizing the power within me. I was entranced by my ancestors and to the courageous warriors, proud of my Māori roots. But there is another side to my Māori inheritance that puts my recognition of our warrior nature into a modern perspective.

The book and movie "Once Were Warriors" depicts the wasteland of urban life, as modern Māori find themselves disconnected from their powerful roots. It reveals the tough reality of the urban Māori, where alcoholism and domestic violence threaten relationships and lives. The British ideals of women beneath men are in stark contrast to the Māori's original way of life. Much of the self-destructive behaviour and gut-wrenching tragedy portrayed within

2 one of the voyaging canoes that carried migrating Polynesians to New Zealand, according to Māori tradition.

3 Tohunga means expert priest, spiritual healer, teacher.

this narrative invoked a frightening truth for me: I was transported back to the violence and abuse of my own childhood.

So many families of my Māori lineage had been drowning in horrific domestic violence, including my family. This deep wound, product of a systematic breakdown of the nature of the original Māori people, was invisible to my non-Māori friends, and as a young girl experiencing this reality first hand, I had no way to express the depth of my anguish. It helped to dive deeper into the lore and spirituality of my strong Māori roots.

My great grandmother, Te Arahori Manunui, came from a long line of *Rangatira*[4]. She was from the tribe Ngati Tuwharetoa. A full-blooded Māori woman, she was one of the women who began the Māori Women's Welfare League in 1951 to support local Māori women throughout the massive changes that colonisation and urbanisation provoked within New Zealand.

Many Māori after World War II moved to the cities for work, leaving behind the strong structure of community life in the tribal lands, becoming dispersed and disorientated in their new urban and suburban setting. The Welfare League was the Māori version of our modern-day 'Women's Circles,' and became an important positive support network for Māori women suddenly worlds away from the rural village life of their tribal lands. Te Arahori was able to help bring support and comfort to Māori women who were struggling in this new foreign world.

I was fortunate to be with my great grandmother a number of times as a small child. She was a soft and gentle woman, with an air of ethereal elegance and poise about her. Her speech was soft and nectar-sweet, her hands velvet-warm. Her hugs were comforting and safe. She had the aspect of a true elder. My sisters and I would linger in her embrace, soaking up the affection we so craved and had in only a very small measure in our own immediate family home.

---

4 Hereditary Spiritual Leaders, chief of the tribe who held great wisdom.

She grew into this elegance over time, over a life of great challenge. Ironically, the cycle of abuse and violence in my family started with the child born to this strong Māori woman out of wedlock.

Her firstborn, my grandfather Derek Tawari O te Rangi Manunui, was the result of her romantic episode with a half-Māori and half-Jewish man, John Atirau (Jack) Asher. She would eventually marry and have other children, but my grandfather grew up feeling lost and insufficient. He had little connection with Jack, his biological father, and was not fully accepted by his stepfather. He never had a man to look up to and learn from.

He found compensation for these weaknesses, as many Māori who once were warriors have, in women and alcohol – a toxic pattern too easily passed on to my father and his other siblings. Though my grandfather would later return to the warmth of his Māori roots and find more purpose, the abusive part of his legacy lived on through his children.

In the playground of my primary school in West Auckland, Pakeha[5] kids teased, and bullied Polynesian and Māori kids like me. I often intervened, threatening to call my much older sister who was in the big kids area if they didn't stop and go away. Usually it worked, and I comforted the children who cried after these incidents.

Even though I was tiny, I was drawn to stand up for other Māori and Polynesian kids, perhaps because I was not able to stand up for myself or sisters at home. I felt a wisp of freedom within the school; a space where my monster, my father, did not hold sway. I was safer there.

Racism was prevalent in West Auckland. I remember a schoolteacher shouting at me for speaking to a Pakeha girl, saying that I

5 Children of European descent.

was distracting her from working. In reality we were both chatting, but this teacher always picked on me. The Māori one.

After another time talking with my Pakeha friend, the teacher ordered me to stand and face the wall because no one wanted to see my 'naughty ugly face. ´ This time I saw clearly that the teacher was bullying me. I didn't turn my face into the corner but stood with my arms crossed over my chest looking directly at the teacher and students.

She came over to scream in my face to '*do as I'm told*' and it seemed like she was going to hit me. I squeezed my eyes shut, preparing for a hit as I did at home, bracing for her strike. She just kept screaming.

A wave of powerful energy surged through me. This was not right and I was not going to adhere to her commands. Eventually she dragged me off by the arm to sit outside the principal's office. Mother was called and she came rushing into the school.

"What is all this fuss about? What happened?" My mother enquired to the principal.

"Your daughter has been causing problems, shouting at the teacher in her classroom. She was not listening and displayed defiant behaviour. We will not tolerate this in the school." The principal sneered at us from behind his desk.

Mother looked at me and asked me why I was shouting. I told her what really happened. My mother was shocked.

"You are trying to blame a seven-year-old child for not listening to an adult teacher who was shouting! My daughter says she did not shout. That means she did not shout. Your teacher was the one shouting at her for not turning her face into the corner of a room. How pathetic, a grown woman shouting at a little girl." Mother defended me.

"Don't you dare come into my office telling me off about my teachers. We don't want people like you here at this school. You bloody Māori are all the same, always causing trouble. Leave my office – leave this school – and don't come back!"

"I don't want my daughters here at your terrible school anyway! We are all happy to leave!" Mother screamed in return.

Mother grabbed my hand, and we spun off out of Don Buck Primary school never to return again.

These episodes of adults and kids being racist were quite common even in the 80s when I was growing up. It surprises me still, coming from a family of mixed Pakeha and Māori heritage, that there could be such racial ignorance in New Zealand.

Even my own Pakeha family used to put down my father and us for being Māori, never missing a chance to note how much blacker my younger sister was than the rest of us.

Spending time in nature provided me great solace from racial discrimination and the abuse. I found my peace in the rustling of leaves, the trees dancing, the wind whispering and the transformational power of water. My sisters were my best friends and we kept joy glowing in our hearts as we explored the natural world around us, outside of the family house of turbulence.

We would sneak over to our neighbour's house where, in his back garden, a bigger jungle-like area gave us the perfect setting for magical adventures. Undetected in our secret jungle it was as if the fairies of the rainforest beckoned us to enjoy the wonders of the natural world, forgetting

the family woes and the racial imbalances of the bigger world for those sacred moments. We hugged trees and lay on the ground feeling happiness together. We had become the magic rainforest fairies of Don Buck Road.

In the Māori tradition, dolphins and whales are ancestors of our people. We have always shared an intimate bond with them since ancient times when the Polynesian people navigated the oceans. Whales and dolphins were guides, and our ancestors swam with them, free and close as family.

As a child on holiday with the family at a beach on the far north island, my sisters and I spent a sun-speckled afternoon swimming in the ocean. Tired and floppy from the exertion of a day with the waves, we had just showered, dressed, and were combing each other's hair outside as we looked to the ocean in front of us. A family of dolphins burst through the surface of the water, jumping and splashing in great fun.

Without any thought, we dropped everything to the ground and ran as fast as we could down to the water. Our hearts raced, excited to meet the dolphin family. With all our clothes on, my sister Iraena and I jumped into the ocean and swam as fast as we could to catch the dolphins. This was the first time that we had witnessed dolphins in the wild, and we were ecstatic.

They were close. We saw a flash of their fins and realised that we were inside a whole pod, it seemed like hundreds of dolphins. They came up to the surface of the water and disappeared again, playing a game of hide and seek with us. Sometimes they came so close that we were within arms-length of them. I stroked my hand on one of the dolphin's backs, her skin dewy like a watermelon. I was overwhelmed with excitement, my heart ready to burst from my chest.

It was as if the dolphins were enjoying playing the game with us, too. We had no fear or inhibition, only the excitement of moving with ease with our new friends in the water. We could hear them talking under the water, their unique clicking sounds were somehow familiar and soothing to our hearts. We spit water from our mouths, spouting like dolphins as we laughed, lost in the moment.

Suddenly, a great heaviness began to weigh us down. Our clothes. We were not dolphins. Wet and heavy, our denim jeans were lead weights on our skinny legs. We swallowed water and gasped for breath; we were going down.

A nearby boat came to our rescue. They saw us panicking to stay afloat and came to help. My sister and I grabbed at our soggy jeans and threw them on board the boat. Though we were urged to get in, we swam away toward the dolphins, eager to return and newly energised now without our weighted jeans. The dolphins resurfaced and came close, then disappeared again. Our hearts thumped like a *djembe* drum as we chased them, exhilarated again by our game. After a time, they swam further than we could follow, and playtime was over.

The rescue boat had kept a watchful eye, and wearily, my sister and I hopped on board. We were safe, and we had just experienced the best moment of our lives. The sun was beginning to set, the skies painting the waves with sparkling light. Jumping out of the boat carrying our wet clothes, we saw mother racing toward us. Even her stream of anxiety-filled recriminations didn't pull us from our dream-like state after the dolphin encounter. We were awash in wonder.

Young Māori warrior children experienced a coming-of-age initiation, left on an island to return to the mainland on their own. It is said that dolphins often assisted these young warriors, giving them safe passage across the water back to shore.

Making it back to the mainland in one piece would mean that the gods and goddesses were watching out for them, and they would live a powerful warrior life. My sister and I, that day, had our dolphin initiation. Now we knew without a doubt that this strong bond with our ocean family was real. We were stronger than when we first entered the water. Changed.

This encounter with the dolphins would be the first of many times that I would swim with the dolphins in the wild, in many countries and in many oceans. I often looked for them, my water family, my calm refuge in tumultuous times. Without fail they would appear.

"I am going to be a vegetarian. I have made my decision and now that I am 13 years old, I can make my own choices."

I proclaimed my new path aloud, half-scared and half-excited.

Half-scared because I had no idea if my father would fly off the rails as was his nature. Half-excited because, after all, I was a teenager now, and I knew with clear conviction what I wanted. I have no idea how I came to believe that turning 13 conferred sudden, magical authority over one's own life, but the belief was strong.

I had just returned from a week visiting a friend and her family. They were all vegetarians, and I loved the food they had prepared. In my own home, I had been forced to eat meat for thirteen years, despite the fact that I had never liked the rubbery taste or the chewy texture in my mouth. In fact, it made me feel sick to my stomach. As I got older and refused to eat the meat put on my plate, my mother would threaten withholding dessert.

Sweets are my most favourite thing, so I devised a daring plan. I would slide the meat off my plate at dinner time and hide it in the napkin resting on my lap. After dinner, I would feed the meat scraps to my cat. It worked rather well, and I went largely undetected.

"What? You stupid girl, you don't know what you're talking about!" My father, with his usual fury, spewed filthy fire-filled words at me.

"You'll just get sick. You'll get even skinnier than you already are. Fucking stupid kid. You'll see. Another of your stupid ideas." His words burnt me deep inside.

I trembled on the inside every time father lashed out, no idea of the size of the storm he would wage on us. He could become enraged at the drop of hat. In our house, it was best to stay quiet. Best not to engage with him, in fear of being blasted. Thirteen years of dreaded meat-eating, and my trust in my newly minted authority, gave me strength to face him in spite of all my expectations.

Now my mother chimed in.

"Don't expect me to make you anything special. You won't get any special treatment in this house. I won't be making you any vegetarian things. What will you eat? Only vegetables?"

"I'll be fine." I rolled my eyes, expecting they would not support my decision anyway.

I was fine, but I was the main target for Father's unending put downs, especially in the kitchen.

"That tofu looks disgusting."

"You won't last eating that crap."

"Just like your stupid Aunty who thinks vegetarian is good. She is just dumb just like you."

Though it hurt deep inside when he growled at me like this, and tears welled up inside, I swallowed my tofu and tears as the lump in my throat grew. I would not allow him to ever see me cry. I would not give him the pleasure to think that he had won. The *I am not good enough story* started in my mother's womb, but the more he insulted me, the more determined I became.

I would make my life very different from his. One day he would see.

My first major life decision was final.

It was that same year of my new teen freedom, when my second eldest sister, Iraena Rama Te Awhina, just two years older than me, came home one night from a party, disorientated and rambling incoherently. She was crying and then angry. Happy and then sad. I could not understand what was going on for her. Maybe her drinks were spiked?

After three days of continued disorientation and lack of sleep, she ran off in a frenzy. We called the police and she was taken away in an ambulance. It was then that she was admitted to the Children's Hospital in Auckland. My parents were in complete disarray, frantic to help her.

She refused to see my parents. Only my younger sister Lainie and I could enter her room. The hospital smelled of stuffy old shoes, the drab cream walls cried misery. After being led through several well-locked doors we saw her. Sitting alone on her bed she had a sombre stare, lost in her pain. It was obvious they had given her a sedative to calm her down. She seemed suspicious, even of her sisters, her best friends. I wanted to hold her tight and tell her everything would be OK, though I hesitated as I did not want to upset her further. Cautious and holding back tears, we waited for the right moment to try to get answers.

She began to tell us a rambling tale about that party. With anger and sadness now written across her face, she told us how she was shoved around by the *'pretty girl'* from school, accused of flirting with the girl's boyfriend, how she was shunned, accused, berated. And I recognized a pattern. This breakdown had a long history.

Our first childhood traumas were the episodes of hearing Father's violence toward Mother. Not once or twice. Often. And then, to our eldest sister, Angie. Mother seemed unable to stop his violence, helpless in the face of it, even to protect her daughter. Angie was shipped off to live with her biological father in Australia. "Too much to handle," they said. This panicked Iraena.

"Will he do that to me?"

None of us understood my father or his violence, but Iraena tried harder than anyone not to aggravate him. She put so much pressure on herself to be the perfect little girl, but in my father's eyes, she was never perfect enough. The trauma of our childhood sat heavy with Iraena, as she imagined the self-imposed burden of suddenly being the eldest daughter.

Iraena was also bullied in school. Despite, or perhaps because of the allure of her intense beauty, other girls relentlessly picked on her. Jealousy, competition, whatever the reason, they found a good target in Iraena because she avoided confrontation, the perfect victim who just wanted to be liked.

One day in high school I caught her crying in the bathroom, defeated by another incident. Hugging her tight I wanted to make everything better. I held back my own tears and told her not to worry. The younger sister, strong and confident, I had assigned myself as her protector from a young age. I might have done something to those girls had Iraena given me their names. She knew how I would react, and in a way, she protected me right back. I never found out who hurt her.

In those days, I tried to distract her with some of my naughty not-so-perfect teenage escapades. For a moment, she would laugh with me. Maybe she would see that she didn't have to be so serious. The recent incident at the party seemed to have broken through some protective shield my sister had built, to insulate herself from the barrage of violence in our household and episodes of bullying at school. It wasn't time, though, to distract her with stories. We sat, listened, and cried with her, hoping this storm would soon pass, and she could come home and we would be together again.

I'll never be fully sure why Iraena was affected so strongly by that incident at the party. She was a sensitive soul and I easily recognised the wounds of our shared family trauma, though we never spoke about it in that way. I might have been aided toward handling this family trauma, just a bit, by a terrible breathing attack that landed me in the emergency room when I was only seven.

All I can remember was my mother racing me into the car. I was in and out of consciousness. I could not speak. Sharp pains tore into my chest and ribs like rusty razors. Mother looked at me through the rear-view mirror, calling my name in desperation to keep me awake. Dizzy, I tried to open my eyes. I felt her arms around me as she carried my limp body, rushing me into the emergency unit.

I was put straight onto a breathing machine. The sharp daggers were now piercing my chest and back. I tried my best to sip in some air, but the pain would not allow me to breathe. I thought this is what dying must be like.

I remember feeling the attentive love from my mother, her voice, her touch. At that moment I would have been happy to die, enveloped in the most warmth she ever gave me. I was never sure if she loved me until her gentle touch and voice confirmed in my little heart what I wondered about every day: She loved me.

"Come on, breathe honey." She forced a smile onto her frightened, tearful face.

For her I breathed. Slow and steady like a timid turtle I managed to sip some oxygen into my lungs. I was bruised and heavy all over, but I was not dead.

Doctors found no real cause for what happened to me that day. They suggested bronchitis or asthma but remained unsure. Still, they prescribed antibiotics, steroids, and asthma inhalers which my mother ignored. She didn't believe this was asthma and looked for an alternative. She had so little experience with illness, growing up on a farm. She never remembered a day when her parents were sick growing up. In later years, her father was diagnosed with cancer in his 60s and she visited him for the first time ever in a hospital. There he seemed to die slowly before her eyes. Hospitals and doctors meant *death* to my mother.

Crazy as it was to visit all the wacky failed attempts at finding an alternative healer, I was happy to be spending one-on-one time with my mother. In a household of so many girls and a monster, it was special to have alone time with her. I was tired of being dragged from one healer to another. This one, though, had a sweet front garden, with tiny blue flowers. I was calm and peaceful as we approached the front door. The house, inside, was fairy-like; bright colours and fabulous fragrances permeated the house, incense mixed with firewood. The healer was soft, not at all like the previous so-called alternative healers we had met. She asked me a few questions.

"Do you sleep well?"

"Do you ever get headaches?"

"Is everything OK at home?"

Her eyes were kind. She looked straight through me, as if she knew everything.

Not knowing what to say about home life, my cheeks blushed red and my eyes dropped to the floor. I did not want to get Mother in trouble. It was really Father who made everything at home *not OK*. Mother was helping me and that was all that mattered. I shyly told her everything was OK.

"Are you sure honey?"

She tried to gently push me further.

How I wanted to tell her everything, that things were not fine, that we lived with a terrible monster. But something inside would not form the words. Embarrassment and shame kept me silent. She smiled and then told me she was going to prepare some special tinctures. I watched her as she measured drops and liquids into small brown bottles.

She took my hand in hers. She asked me if I wanted to learn a simple breathing technique. Her hands were warm and kind.

"Breathe in, one…two… three… four… five."

I tried my best to follow.

"Hold your breath now, one…two… three… four… five."

"Now, exhale, one….two… three… four… five."

She counted as I held my breath for the final five counts. We continued this way as her gentle hands held mine and I looked out the window to her colourful garden. I could breathe peace with ease, somehow I felt lighter. I wanted to stay in her magical space forever.

I used this breathing technique often throughout my childhood and youth and know this helped me survive some of the traumas of family life. I would recognise these breathing techniques in the Yoga training and healing arts practises I discovered in my later teens. Yoga would become a saving grace in my life and the beginning of a lifetime dedication to the wisdoms of India. My breathing problems went away as I practised, the breath of life was now my friend. My first *Pranayama*[6], my first yoga practice. By seven, I was onto something.

Tihei Mauri ora.

6 Breathing exercises of the ancient Yoga systems India.

Back in the hospital at my sister's bedside, I was a stormy, furious ocean seeing my sister suffering again. I couldn't protect her from her bullies. Then came a diagnosis: bipolar.

"What does that mean? No, I don't believe you. What do you people know? You can't label my daughter. She won't take medicine. She doesn't even need medicine. When will she come home? I want her to come home now. She is my daughter. I want her to come home now!"

My mother poured forth with a stream of desperation.

The shock and disbelief in the car on the way home was palpable. My mother was full of pain and anguish, my father angry and uncontrollable, profanity punctuating every sentence. They blamed anything and everything: the party she was at, the school, the kids, the doctors. Never turning inward to see their own part in the drama.

As we arrived home, Mother looked at me with anguish filled eyes.

"She will be OK, right? Will she be OK ? Everything will be OK , right?" She whimpered desperately.

I hugged her tight and said what she wanted to hear. I did not believe it one bit. I was my mother's protector, too – my own self-imposed burden to shoulder.

But who protected me?

I knew that as long as Mother decided to keep us living with Father the monster, there was no way that things were going to be OK. Nothing would be OK if she insisted on keeping my sisters and me within this dark home.

I was experimenting with drugs and alcohol, spending carefree time with friends, and eventually at 15 getting my driver's licence. I made a series of free-spirited road trips around the North Island of New Zealand, and without a care in the world, my friends became family. I was finally free of the toxic home life that chained me through my childhood years.

We slept in the car, on the beach under the stars, in someone's home, or anywhere the wind took us. Nothing stood in our way, and even if it did – with my girlfriends we met it head on, rebels without a cause.

I couldn't stay on the road forever, though. I could not stand living with my father. I wanted better for myself, for my sisters, for my mother. I needed to protect myself first and foremost, so I moved into an apartment with friends, working at a local supermarket while still going to school.

I was free and ready to support myself, but soon found it was far from paradise. Night after night, teenagers coming and going, no rules, no boundaries, and it wasn't long before my health suffered miserably. I was exhausted most of the time. My energy levels dropped. The house was a huge mess, a permanent smog of cigarette smoke. No amount of breathing exercises seemed to calm me out of this – my breathing problems came back with a vengeance.

My mother came to visit and I wanted her to scoop me out of this nightmare and take me home. She laid into me right away.

"How can you live in such a place? You must come home immediately! I knew this was a bad idea from the start. This is terrible."

My desperation turned to annoyance – with her. I couldn't admit defeat. I couldn't go back to the monster, my father, and anyway, how could *she* stand to live with him? My ego stood firm. I was right and she was wrong – to stay with such a man and put her daughters through so much stress and trauma.

It was only after confiding with my friend who felt the chaos there, too, that I acted on my desire to leave this twisted fantasy of independence. It wasn't a weakness; it wasn't giving up. My friend and I realised we needed support, and hard as it was to go home, imperfect as that support would be, it would, for now, come from our parents. We were ready to go home.

Given the perspective of those few wild months, home was different this time. My father was in the *I told you so mode*, but I managed to keep my attitude neutral. My mother stayed quiet, and I retreated downstairs to my old bedroom. Mother had changed the sheets on the bed, the comforting sound of Tui birds floated in through my bedroom window. Everything was crisp, clean, and quiet in my room.

For that moment at least, for the first time in a very long time, I was happy to be home. Prison or no prison. Monster or no monster. My comfortable bed was all that mattered, and I crashed out hard under the soft, silky covers.

Fly free

It did not take long before the demon storm returned, and my comfortable home ceased to be a sanctuary. Father shouting at Mother, putting her down, disgusted at anything from hair in the bathroom sink to the washing machine being overused. Every time anyone of us sisters appeared in the kitchen he would fume.

"What are you doing now? You better not be eating everything. Stop making such a mess, you better fucking clean up or you will be sorry."

His hissing words made me tremble.

Long days turned into weeks staying over at girlfriends' homes. Time with my friends was the best escape from my family house. When I did come home to get fresh clothes and some of Mother's baked goods, I would get a chance to catch up with my sisters.

Iraena and I shared the same floor of the house, our bedrooms opposite one another. When things became unbearable in the house with Father yelling and Mother whining, we would escape onto the terrace that joined our rooms. Rolling our eyes at the pathetic parents carrying on as usual, we would have a good catch-up on our boyfriends and girlfriends. The only things I missed about being at home were my sisters.

Listening to the peaceful *Morepork ruru*[7] from the rainforest below our house, we could, for a moment, be birds again, safe in the forest as the house above dissolved away.

Growing up in *Aotearoa*[8] we were enveloped in an enchanting natural environment. My first spiritual connection came through the temple of nature, in every ocean wave, river and waterfall, in each rainforest tree, in the rustling of leaves and in the gentle breeze that brushed my cheeks. The nature of New Zealand is powerful and potent.

For as long as I can remember, nature enveloped me in light. Not metaphorical light – real light.

I didn't know what the golden rainbow lights were, or why they came to me. As a child, I had no reference for spiritual experience. I only knew that within the warmth of these lights, I remained protected, as if love flowed from the lights into my body. Whether my eyes were open or closed, the colours and light would swirl in and around me. My secret saviour in the midst of the strife in my home, the light came to me without summoning, without expectation. My heart was at ease in the lights. They would follow me around the world; my secret protection.

All my life I wanted to travel. I always knew that when I came of age, I would be off to discover the world. It would be a perfect escape to get far away on the other side of the planet safe from the monster's scorn to allow my spirit to finally fly free. The further the better.

When I was 18, my world-wide adventures began. I bought flights to Thailand where I would stay with my uncle, my mother's brother who had a home in Bangkok. I was so excited with my escape plan ready. Nothing would stop me from opening to a new way of life.

---

7 Native New Zealand owl

8 A Māori name for New Zealand

My parents and sisters came to the airport to see me off. As I left to board, I turned around to see my mother crying, sad and happy at the same time. I had made the ultimate escape. My sisters cried happy tears. My father had the same despondent look he always had, uninterested and annoyed at something or nothing.

I did not show them any tears, only exhilaration to be leaving. As soon as I was out of their sight, I broke into tears, torrents down my cheeks. I leaned against the wall of the jetway and collapsed to the floor. I cried for my family, for all the pain, for everything. For my freedom from the madness at home, for fear for the first time away from my family, for triumph that I had taken my time to fly away, for compassion for my parents' failure to show me love, recognition of their limits. I cried for it all.

I would miss my sisters too much, my best friends my whole life. We were each other's saving grace in our traumatic times in childhood. I had no idea what I was to embark upon, though I knew for certain that I was ready. Every morning I awakened with a desire to learn more about the world and its people, outside of my blue flower-patterned walls of my bedroom. Now I was on my way and ready, ready to fly free.

I had no idea that going to Thailand was going to have such a huge impact on my life, it was to be so much more than just fun and adventure. My life path and purpose was about to take shape.

Bangkok and Buddha

TOUCHING DOWN IN BANGKOK, I was delighted by the tropical warmth. As soon as the aeroplane doors opened, sultry heat and the scent of cigarettes hit me, and instant contentment that I was miles away from New Zealand. I jumped into a taxi and gave the driver some rough directions to my uncle's home in downtown Bangkok.

In those days there was no Google Maps, yet somehow the taxi managed, relying on vast experience and collective wisdom. The driver asked people on the streets for information as we neared where he thought we were going. I was amazed when a crowd of eight people gathered around the taxi, greeting us with hands together in prayer at their hearts. Looking at us with such affection, I had no idea who they were or what they wanted. Then out of nowhere in the middle of the street, a handsome young Thai man appeared on the scene, all smiles, and beckoned the taxi into the driveway.

We had arrived. My uncle was not at home, but the young man welcomed us inside. He was my uncle's boyfriend, Watee, and the people who had gathered around our car were local neighbours, advised of my arrival, whom I would get to know over the next few months.

"Sa wa de ka. Sa wa de ka."

Everyone was greeting us in their native tongue, and I was captivated straight away. The beautiful form of Thai greeting, bowing and honouring each other, felt so natural and so good. I took to it right away, and quickly adopted it as my own.

In his very broken English Watee managed to speak,

"I Watee, your uncle good man, you my friend OK? Come OK?"

He showed me to my room in the upper part of the house and carried my giant bags up the stairs. He was a tiny skinny guy, but very strong. I settled in and lay down on the bed, buzzing. Exhausted and excited to be in Thailand, ready for the journey to unfold. I could not wait to discover Bangkok and begin my adventure.

The very next day in a tuk tuk ride around the city, I encountered such movement: cars, people, pollution and tuk tuks everywhere, the heat of the smog, the horns beeping in every tone imaginable. Chaotic as it was, I was happy with the mayhem. We arrived at our first destination, *Wat Phra Kaew* in the heart of Bangkok, *the Temple of the Emerald Buddha.* As we walked in to buy our tickets, I was ushered off to the side and made to wrap a long sarong over my bare legs.

First lesson - hotpant shorts would not be appropriate in the temples.

As I entered the temple complex, a rush of excitement washed over me, taking me back in time. The impressive architecture and bright colours of red and green and yellow were shining exquisite in the morning sun. Like a little child in wonder, eyes wide, I wanted to run everywhere to see every corner of the temple, its beauty was jewel-like. Unlike anything I had seen before.

Everyone in the temple was invited to place an offering of incense and candles at the altars. A mix of monks and everyday people, tourists and locals alike. There didn't seem to be much order, but somehow it worked. A warm welcome followed us in these temples, a sense of acceptance quite unlike the feelings of judgement that pervaded church gatherings in New Zealand. There, I was always trying and always failing to do the right thing within a very strict, rigid set of rules that held little sense for me. Here there was no hierarchy, but rather an inviting space, no prying eyes awaiting my next terrible mistake.

Every morning in Thailand I awakened excited like a small child on the morning of her birthday, anticipating the next visit to a sacred temple site as a gift. The Buddhist temples of Bangkok are ancient wonders, and I was enraptured by them, and by the ceremonies I witnessed, the meditation and mindfulness.

Prior to my visit to Thailand, what I knew of Buddhism was anecdotal. My friend's mother was a Buddhist, and I admired her. I had heard that Tina Turner was a Buddhist. It sounded like a kind yet fashionable way. In Thailand, though, I became attracted to Buddhism beyond the observable. The Buddha's teachings landed in my head and my heart.

I found myself daydreaming, lost in contemplation of the Buddhist way of life. Day and night, I studied the Buddha's teachings through books. In particular *'The four noble truths,'* the foundational Buddhist teachings. I immersed myself in thought around these four truths.

1) The truth that suffering exists

2) The origin of all suffering

3) The cessation of suffering -no longer suffering

4) The true liberated path away from suffering

As I was drawn toward an incipient understanding of Buddhist precepts, my adventure became more than a usual tourist's vacation. I could not stop thinking about these simple yet profound truths. I found deep resonance with them, from deep inside, and they added context to my journey. My life to this point had been family trauma and suffering, so while I had lived the first two truths, the second two were intriguing.

Can one truly transcend all suffering? If it was true, then this was all I wanted to achieve in life.

I wanted to run away and dive into understanding these four noble truths -- upside down and backwards. After so much suffering in my life, to understand suffering this way, as a truth and something that could be understood on a spiritual level – made sense to me. While wildly different from anything I had known, it seemed so familiar. My heart was buzzing with excitement to learn more.

I spoke to the locals about Buddha, and in their broken English they tried their very best to help me understand. They spoke of compassion. They spoke of no need to suffer any longer. They spoke of Buddhist topics with such grace, so easy to digest and comprehend.

There was no fanaticism or rigour like with the Christians I met in New Zealand: their way or the highway. The Buddhist way was relaxed and inclusive. I was astounded; I could feel myself changing deep in my core. The changes I started to feel were natural and easy for me. I began to meditate every day. I chanted Buddhist chants. I went to the temples and sat for hours. Time stood still. I was living in another era. My life as a young kiwi girl faded away, along with much of the weight of my childhood suffering.

"I am going to become a monk."

With pride I revealed to my uncle my new plan for life.

"What? Don't you mean a nun? You a nun! Ha! You crazy girl."

Uncle scoffed at the idea.

"I mean it, I am serious, I want to spend the rest of my life as a Buddhist monk. I am going to speak with one of the Buddhist nuns tomorrow. You will see."

I left my uncle babbling as he continued to laugh at my idea. Undisturbed, I retreated upstairs.

The next day, a nun welcomed me to the temple, and led me to a quiet space with small wooden benches. Incense wafted in along the corridors. I could hear chanting in the distance. I was excited and nervous. She had such an aura of peace and tranquillity about her. I hoped she wouldn't hear my self-judgments and my un-peaceful mind. When she spoke I heard compassion in her soft words, and I relaxed a little. When I spoke, she listened to me fully. I had never in my life been so fully heard, and with such an absence of judgement.

I asked her many questions about life in the temple, about the Buddha and the four noble truths. She answered me with kindness and warmth. I was open to the emergence of my true spiritual path. Without a trace of doubt, I was ready to give up my mundane life and share it with devotees like this Buddhist nun.

"We all must cut off our hair."

She took clear note of my long, long golden-brown hair.

"Oh, um, really?" I was shocked.

My hair was an expression of myself for all my 18 years, in all its rainbow colours, with all its braided and curled and then smooth-again textures.

"Shave it all off?" I asked with a sweetness hoping that she might reconsider this rule.

"Yes, all off. Like this," she replied, smiling and rubbing her shiny bald head.

My dreams of becoming a Buddhist monk were obliterated in that smooth motion of her hand across her scalp. I wondered for a moment what her hair might have looked like. My heart sank into my chest. I was not ready for being bald. I couldn't be Sinead O'Connor.

I left the temple deflated and shattered. I was too attached to my hair. Would I miss this opportunity of surrender to a dedicated Buddhist life just because I could not let go of my hair? Usually, I set my mind to something, and nothing would take me off course. But baldness was not in the plan. Feeling silly and selfish, and suddenly detoured, I made my way back to my uncle's home.

Arriving there, my uncle and his friends were already baked on whiskey and beer and God knows what else. My uncle slurred a few snide remarks, elated that things had not gone to plan for me and my '*Mother Teresa idea.*'

For him, it was cause for more celebration and downing another drink. I ignored him and retreated to my room. More than ever, I was fixated on the Buddha's teachings, leaving me more questions than answers: What was my way out of this material suffering? If I could not be a monk, then how would I realise these ultimate truths?

What next? How will I ever release my suffering?

One evening to my surprise, some of our local neighbours stopped by, friends of my uncle's boyfriend Watee.

"*Sa wa dee ka.*" We all exchanged Thai greetings as they came in bowing to one another.

They brought countless bags of vegetables and cooking utensils. One woman brought a gas cooker. Good thing Watee appeared, as I had no idea they were coming over to visit, unsure what was going on I enquired to Watee what was going on.

"Come, come we sit up. OK?" Watee ushered us all upstairs.

"Time for party." He grinned cheekily.

We went upstairs to a terrace that I had not seen before. The neighbours set up the cooker and started to prepare the fresh vegetables. I was astounded. In western countries it was unusual for neighbours to turn up unannounced with a full kitchen, a bag of groceries, and a whole bunch of uninvited guests, but once I got over my surprise, it was nice and homey to have this activity on the terrace.

They started pulling out pots and pans and preparing the gas cooker. I sat with a couple of the women and asked if I could help prepare some vegetables, but they declined. They wanted me to relax. I sat with them, observing their small, delicate hands preparing vegetables with such skill, all the while giggling and smiling, immersed in a joyous mood. In no time at all, we were eating the most delicious vegetarian *pad thai.*

They remembered that I was vegetarian and thoughtfully made sure that this evening's feast was suitable. These tasty dishes kept on coming. More vegetables and tofu. Some were super-spicy burn-your-tongue dishes. Others like pure papaya passion in my mouth. It was the best Thai food I had ever eaten, seasoned as it was, with the kindness and love from these village people. It struck me how

Thai people are playful and full of joy, no matter what their age or material circumstance. They radiated a natural exuberance.

The food was infused with traditional Thai spices and their love. We sat on the terrace giggling, unable to communicate in words, enjoying the universal language of love and service and food! A bubbling of humility stirred my heart. These neighbours lived in tiny one-room box homes next to my uncle's grand house. They had nothing, but the greatest wealth belonged to them, in the Buddha's teachings and kind, loving, compassionate hearts, ready and willing to serve others with no expectation.

The big city life of Bangkok was wearing on me. I wanted to see more, to get out of the noisy, polluted city and see the *real* Thailand in its nature and countryside. A part of me wanted to get away from everything and everyone: the late-night parties, the drinking, the drinking. Watee was excited when he learned that I wanted to travel around his country. He insisted on taking me to his village, on our way to Koh Samet Island. It was agreed we would leave the following day. I was elated to be leaving Bangkok.

Hoping for an authentic Thai experience, we hopped on a local bus. The bus smelled like a mixture of animals and sweat and seemed that it had never been cleaned. I didn't care. I was happy to be on the road, adventuring again to new places. People-watching on the bus, I saw parents with their kids in tow, young boys and girls with butterfly eyes, elderly people slowly making their way through the day, dusty sandals and sure gaze. Innocent and happy like little children. Not an artificial joy, but a true deep honest joy. A humble innocence radiated from the Thai people.

In the middle of a sea of rice paddy fields, Watee said we had arrived. We seemed to be nowhere at all. Climbing down from the bus, my bags were already removed from underneath. I looked around for Watee, but he had disappeared without a trace. After what seemed like an eternity in the sweltering heat, without knowing where I was, or where he was. Suddenly, I saw a small figure on a motorbike approaching. Watee.

"Watee. Where have you been? What is going on? Not good." I was clearly annoyed.

"OK OK , no no, you happy! OK?"

He had obtained a motorbike from somewhere and was urging me to climb on behind him.

"Ummm, what about the luggage, Watee? This is ridiculous. Have you seen my bags?"

I pointed at the bags. I was sweating furiously. It would be madness to fit both of us and all my luggage on that bike.

"No no worry, be OK, happy OK ." He smiled a mischievous grin, which only slightly melted my bubbling temper.

I let go for a moment and surrendered to Watee. He grabbed one bag, I grabbed the other, and by some great miracle we squeezed ourselves and the bags in between on the bike and were off. No helmets, the sun blazing down on us and the wind blasting our faces. We were clutching at each other on that rickety motorbike, my butt aching with every bump. I was hungry, thirsty, had heat exhaustion and my hair kept blowing into my eyes and mouth.

Was he lost? Had I been foolish to trust in him in the first place? Was he angry with my uncle and now seeking revenge by taking me into the middle of nowhere? An array of erratic thoughts flooded my wind-blustered head. I had had enough of this adventure.

Then he stopped, again in the middle of nowhere, in the middle of rice fields. The bumps and ruts of that long road killed any patience I might have mustered.

"What is going on Watee? I am tired. I need water. No good. No good!" I whined.

"OK , OK good come, come OK " He urged me into the field, looking at me timidly.

Across an expanse of dense field, I saw a small dwelling in the distance. We trudged through the growth, and as we approached the thatched hut, a withered man emerged, and embraced Watee with great affection, enfolding him into his arms. Tears streaming from their eyes, they were all smiles. The man invited us into their home, a great relief from the relentless heat. A very small woman sat on the floor. She got up from her small cooker to embrace us, smiling over and over again.

"My Papa! My Mama!"

Watee giggled and smiled like a Cheshire cat.

His parents giggled and smiled too. They hugged, they cried, they laughed. Soon we were all giggling and smiling. After mercifully tracking down bottled water for us, Mama offered us a bowl of rice with fresh chillies on the side. We sat on the floor of the hut and ate this simple offering, as Watee's parents watched my every bite, intent on my satisfaction.

Before I had finished my last bite, admittedly quickly for the hunger that groaned at me, Mama was already offering me more. I was delighted to eat as much as possible. With tears in her eyes, Mama started to talk. I knew no Thai and Watee knew very little English. But he tried his best to translate bits here and there.

"She is so happy you are good people. Your uncle good man. So happy, so good. You stay here."

Mama was smiling and crying at the same time. Just moments ago, I had been suspicious of Watee, this kind young village man. I was feeling terrible to have had such thoughts about him. There was such love and care in his family's home. After the delicious simple meal, we sat again, this time in silence. Mama took my hands in hers and spoke to me. She gazed into my eyes; her own eyes sparkled. Lines of life lessons decorated her wisdom-filled glance.

Our souls were speaking. I had no idea what she was saying, but my heart bubbled with love. She placed a small Buddha pendant into my hand. At her touch, I recalled my great grandmother, Te Arahori Manunui, when I spent time with her as a child in the tribal lands of Taupo. It was like butterflies blessing my heart.

In those few hours, I felt more welcomed and safer than I had before in anyone's home. In an instant, Watee's family became my family. Loving-kindness wasn't so common in the suburbs of West Auckland. I could not tell her with words, how she made my heart sing, the feelings I wanted to share with her, the love and gratitude I wanted to express, but I trusted she could hear me.

As we prepared to leave, I melted into her embrace and cried tears of love and gratitude. She patted my back, and it was so healing: She was a mother as I had imagined mothers, compassionate and kind. This was the mother I had hoped for growing up, when I cried myself to sleep during those demon storms. A simple pat on the back would have been so simple, so healing.

This moment would remain with me forever, etched deep into my heart. As we left Watee's parents standing on the side of the road, I carefully turned around on our crammed motorbike, smiling at them one last time. I could feel their eyes on us as we drove off into the late afternoon. With tears now tracing rivulets on my wind-chapped cheeks, I carried a new peace inside.

Yoga life and banking

On my return to New Zealand after three months in Thailand, I was 19 years old, and most of my friends were starting businesses or going off to university. I had no desire for these things. After Thailand and my introduction to the teachings of the Buddha, after experiencing the generosity of spirit among the people of Thailand, I was changed.

I had come close to a kind of inner peace, and I didn't want that connection to become buried in the *cool* life that I was falling back into. The self-absorption that I lived previously, between one wild party and another, began to give way to more introspection and space for compassion. I wanted to be around compassionate people, who sought a deeper spirituality.

Yoga pointed the way. I had been interested in Yoga since my teenage years, and found the breathing exercises and postures helped me with my anxiety, connecting me to a calm space. A Yoga teacher training course started just down the road from my parents' house, and I saw this as an auspicious sign. I saw a clear connection between Yoga and the Buddhist practises I was drawn to in Thailand: Before the Buddha became enlightened, he followed the path of Yogic practises. For me they were intimately connected.

My friends thought I was crazy. People told me I could do much better than to study Yoga, and that other, bigger, better opportunities lie ahead. The more my friends said that I should not study Yoga, the more I knew it was meant to be. Now I was a rebel *with* a cause, inspired to be a top student for the first time in my life.

Yoga is like a tree. It has a core trunk and many branches. To mention just a few, there is the Yoga of the mind, Yoga for the body, Yoga in relationship to cause and effect, Yoga of devotion Bhakti Yoga[9], Yoga of music and dance. The word Yoga means "to unite." The mind, body and spirit become synchronised in harmony as the holy trinity of balance and unity.

The Buddha originally came from India and practised many of the ancient Yoga branches before he reached the state of *Samadhi*[10], a state of supreme bliss where all aspects of one's mind, body, mental, emotional, spiritual are united, leading to enlightenment. This spoke strongly to me, and after my experiences in Thailand I was keen to dive deeper into the heart of these ancient wisdoms.

In a Yoga studio not far from my home, I discovered a beautiful sanctuary overlooking the rainforest and the Pacific Ocean. During a year-long Yoga teacher training with a Dutch instructor trained in the *Iyengar* style of Yoga, I let go of my life-long distrust of teachers, inspired by her discipline and the discipline she instilled in her pupils.

I was young, and – not having fully left the party girl behind – I often came to class hungover. On these days, the Sanskrit chants made me dizzy, and *asana*[11] exercises tied me up in knots. Our group would have to go over and over the chants until we had a full run through with no mistakes. I was usually the one messing up, the one with a fuzzy head. This was serious business, and the teacher was not there to pamper our egos.

She would go hard on me these days, push me to the point of sweat and tears, upside down balancing on my head with my legs bound in lotus position – and then instruct me to breathe. Painful as it was, I knew this ancient practice was my saving grace. So, I

9 See endnotes

10 Sanskrit term used to explain an enlightened state of inner union.

11 Sanskrit term used for posture in Yoga, which means seat.

breathed. I kept going. It was a necessary purification process. My late-night partying eventually fell away. I would still dance at the parties, but always made sure I was sober and home early. I became very disciplined in my Yoga practice. I did my homework and went beyond. I practised Yoga every day, several hours a day. I read books and studied hard.

'*Ishwara Prana Dhan*' - Patanjali Yoga Sutra[12]

Dedicate your life breath to the divine.

That was all I had left. Hope in this one sutra.

The mind-body-soul equilibrium I experienced was profound. On days my father picked me up from the class, I was able to block out his negativity as we drove home. I was in an altered state of consciousness, a natural bliss-bubble. For the first time I had some lasting tools beyond the breathing exercises I learnt as a child, thanks to the ancient Yoga wisdoms of India.

Content as I was to be learning Yoga, I trusted that the wider world could present me with many more teachers and inspiring people. I was eager to travel again and to open myself to learning from other great spiritual traditions. I had enough indications from having worked in a local bank that the corporate life was not for me.

I was the youngest employee there. The older women working there were very well presented, fashion-conscious, complete with gold jewellery and manicures. Yet most of them seemed to be going through mental and physical problems. They took headache pills every day to cope with daily stress.

Many of them started to open up to me about the issues they were going through. I could see how they were suffering day to day. I could see that money and its trappings were not affording them happiness. Just the opposite. They became embittered in the daily grind of their work. I didn't imagine I'd find teachers here... but sometimes teachers show you what you *don't* want to go towards.

---

12 The Patanjali Yoga Sutras are a collection of ancient Sanskrit Yoga wisdoms of theory and practice of Yoga. Refers to1:23 in the Yoga Sutra.

An aggravating incident at the bank helped illustrate to me how toxic a workplace can be – and I found myself contemplating the meaning of true happiness, as a result.

A customer accused me of short-changing her on a currency conversion, and began to scream. I had calculated carefully, and tried my best over the customer's insults, to show her the conversion. I went to the head teller, Katie, who had worked at the bank for over 30 years. The bank was her whole life. She lived and breathed this bank. And – she did not like me from the moment I joined.

This was her opportunity to put me in my place.

Immediately taking the angry customer's side, she proclaimed my inexperience, and sneered at me through coffee-stained teeth.

"Please, Katie, if you would just check my calculations, you will see that there is no discrepancy." I tried to keep my fiery annoyance inside.

"Don't tell me what to do. You stay back so I can fix your mess."

She shoved me behind her. That shove nearly tipped me over the edge. I was boiling. Katie punched the calculator and then stared at the screen. Once. Twice. She failed to see any problem. I had not committed any mistake. She cleared her throat.

"I am sorry, Madame, it seems that this is the correct amount."

I was livid. How dare they insult me and put me down without reason and without apology. The rage was about to be given voice, and I let it go. I shouted at both of them. I told them off, with my righteous, indignant young *how-dare-you* rage. When I had spewed out everything inside that needed to be said I spun around to leave the area. The staff within the bank looked at me in shock.

As I stormed off to the employee's lunch area, another woman I worked with whispered in my ear.

"Good on you, she had it coming to her, I bet she didn't expect that."

I had never in my life stood up for myself like that and never unleashed such fury. Part of me was excited and liberated. The other part was dreading the consequences.

Though we eventually made peace, this incident had a huge impact on my contentment at the bank. Watching my colleagues equally discontented but plugging away, I realised that I didn't have to be like them. Katie and my co-workers were a different kind of teacher. I didn't want to end up like them.

I found myself contemplating a path to happiness that didn't include soul-less work. I knew that I would not be working much longer in this environment where stress and anxiety took centre stage. I knew that my life could be so different, so much more than what I experienced in that bank. I had no idea what, exactly. I just knew that simply making money was not enough. I was desperate to find another way, and ready and open to explore different ways to think about life and happiness and the future.

Who are the happiest people in the world and why?

What choices can I make to dance life with more joy, to let my true voice sing?

> *"Our deepest fear is not that we are inadequate. Our deepest fear is that we are powerful beyond measure."*
>
> – *Marianne Williamson*

After completing my Yoga Teacher training, I met Nita, a gorgeous middle-aged New Zealand woman, the embodiment of the divine feminine, a gorgeous Goddess. She was confident and comfortable in her skin, a role model for me: the empowered woman, sensual and seductive, strong yet soft. She held herself with such beauty, charm, and grace. I was excited to be around her.

I was 19 at the time, still immature and uncomfortable in my own skin. Nita gave me Taoist books to read, in particular Tantric books on sacred sexuality; how sex can either give us life or drain life from us. I had always embraced my sexuality, and to put it in a sacred context made sense. In essence, Tantra practices *use the body and mind to reach soulful liberated states of consciousness and awareness.*

In ancient cultures worldwide, the most revered Tantric teachers are women. Brought up in a household of four women, I was accustomed to watching my father degrade and demean women as inferior. That the ancients held women in such esteem was eye-opening and just what I needed to hear at the time.

Through this intriguing ancient practice, I added another branch to my tree of Yoga. Tantra, vast and deep, cannot be grasped by the logical mind. With love and respect at the centre, sexuality becomes enlightening. Sex education classes in West Auckland schools didn't teach sex as sacred. Nita became my first Tantric teacher, teaching me the ways of sacred touch with healing energy and the power of the feminine. Most mornings we would sit together and sip tea in her beautiful home overlooking the expansive Pacific Ocean. The only sound is our breath, inhale... exhale...inhale...

The breathing practice and stillness generated powerful surges of energy up my spine and through my body. These practices were safe and empowering with a woman like Nita. Full of energy, I was bubbling and blossoming into my twenties. For the first time in my life I met a woman who knew her self-worth and her power as a woman, a teacher I felt comfortable following. This would be the beginning of a lifelong practice of Tantric sacred sexuality, and the beginning of my journey towards women's empowerment.

Egypt and Mount Sinai

I HAD BEEN SAVING MY money from work at an interior design company – more creative and more relaxed than bank work – and was ready to use it for the next travel adventure. The time had come again to spread my wings and fly.

I heard stories of Cleopatra growing up, how she bathed in milk and honey. I dreamed of floating in a pool of pure bliss, just like her. I was fascinated by the pyramids and daydreamed about living in ancient Egypt. Finally, the time had come for this trip of a lifetime to Egypt.

When we approached the Great Pyramids in the taxi I could not believe the size of them. Man-made mountains glowed on the horizon, icons of an advanced civilization. I was enraptured by the scale of these great structures. Standing at the foot of these pyramids and looking up, I mused. What were the ancient Egyptians thinking when they created these monumental masterpieces? How were these ancient people inspired to contribute so much to this creation? What must this monument have meant to the royal people and regular town people?

A project of this enormity would have required full dedication of humans and God, the power coming together for a cause. In *Te reo Māori,* the ancient New Zealand language, we say *'Kotahitanga'* – together united as one, we can achieve greatness. The pyramids were a solid example of this.

Monuments of this magnitude are spellbinding. It was as if the Gods had come down personally to help them build, with their very own hands. It seemed impossible to me that these pyramids were built by sheer human strength. I saw ancient technology at work, along with divine intervention of their all-powerful Gods. This is one of the greatest mysteries of all time. Some of the most intelligent seekers in history were immersed in trying to solve and unlock the Egyptian mysteries. To this day, many still seek answers, studying the Egyptian past, hoping to unlock even one of the many great secrets here.

I climbed up some of the massive stone slabs that form the pyramid. I closed my eyes and beautiful waves of energy swam through my body. I was immersed in a deep gratitude and contentment. After a lifetime of reading about Egypt, her Gods and Goddesses, the Pharaohs and Queens, I experienced something familiar here, bubbling in my mind and heart.

I was jolted from my reflections by my guide. My guide who, of course, was descended from the Pharaohs, who wouldn't stop talking, who spun stories that contradicted the real history I knew of Egypt, who interfered with my deep appreciation of the ruins by being just a little too close. I had purchased a package tour at the urging of my family and friends and beyond my better judgement. I didn't need the guide – I was an undercover wild warrior woman on a mission to know in person what I had already dreamed. But he was part of the deal so I grit my teeth.

It was time to go inside the Great Pyramid of Giza. There isn't solid evidence on the age of the pyramids. The Great Pyramid is said to contain around 5.9 million tonnes of stone. The pyramid aligned to true north with near-perfect astronomical precision. The three pyramids at the Giza area line up with the three stars in Orion's belt constellation. How the Egyptians accomplished extraordinary calculations and precise alignments tickled my imagination.

We climbed to the main entrance of the Great Pyramid of Giza. My heart was racing in excitement and wonderment as I was to realise my dream. With honour and reverence, I paused, thanking the guardians of this sacred site. The shade of the inner sanctuary of the pyramid provided a welcome relief from the scorching sun.

An evocative aroma of ancient sand and candle flames accompanied us as we descended a small passage into the heart of the pyramid, the stones on either side perfectly cut, so smooth it felt as if they were cut just days ago. I ran my hand across this ancient stone, imagining how many hands would have touched this same spot. I was suspended in time, enveloped in stillness. The guide asked me if I wanted to go all the way inside. Yes, absolutely, I wanted to descend all the way deep into the pyramid.

We came to a small room. We were inside the main tomb. A massive granite sarcophagus rested in the centre of the tomb. After an exchange with my guide, the guard at the door to this tomb started moving people out. I gave the guide some money to pay the tomb guard. Suddenly I was alone with the guide.

"I got you a private tour inside the Great Pyramid." My guide grinned, sidling closer to me.

"Do you want to lay down inside the sarcophagus?" He took hold of my hand as he motioned the way towards the sarcophagus.

All of a sudden my protective senses ignited. How dare this man touch my hand and tell me what I will do. Touching women in public is forbidden in Egypt. I knew I was in a sacred place and had to hold myself together in the face of this man's inappropriate behaviour, but I responded with the strength of the Pharaoh Cleopatra, empowered.

"What I want is for you to get out of this space now and wait outside. Get out." I stared at him until he turned and left. He said something to the tomb guard, and they left me alone.

Alone at last, I stood next to the sarcophagus and came into a Taoist standing meditation stance. I closed my eyes and within moments healing golden light descended and flowed into me, rushing through the top of my head like a waterfall. The energy swirled around me. Stars flashed past as if I was travelling at the speed of light.

My heart was on fire, as if it were pumping into the entire pyramid, absorbed into eternity. I was drawn back into my body as I heard voices speaking in Arabic, my meditation suddenly over. I rejoined with my guide, and in a trance stayed quiet as we made our way out of the Great Pyramid of Giza, in a state of pure bliss and oblivious to his ranting. I was thankful for using my strength to get past him and into the part of the pyramid that took me on a journey to the stars.

An ocean of gratitude wrapped me fully in this moment, as my dream of going deeper into another spiritual tradition unfolded. I had flown with the stars. This ancient Egyptian wisdom revealed itself to me, and in this moment I knew without any doubt that we are made of star light. That the soul *exists* and we are so much more than the physical body. We are light.

Back with the packaged tour, I was with a group of ill-spoken, rowdy young English and Irish tourists, ready to drink their way through the country, starting each day with a hangover. I had to find my own way to get what I wanted from each day, as our group visited a variety of ancient sacred sites and temple palace ruins.

Each time we arrived at a site, I would take note of the hour we were to meet back at the bus and then would slip away from the group undetected, heading to the quiet corners of temples to sit, to pray, and meditate. Lighting a candle and incense that I brought in my backpack, I sat in quiet contemplation of these sacred places.

My meditations were deep, sometimes so deep I had no idea how long I spent in my quiet corner. In these spaces I encountered great peace. The fear and anxiety that gripped me during so much of my life seemed to float off into the distant sands. The prayers and answers came every time, God was with me. I was alone, yet never alone. Safety and protection washed over me.

I often found myself jolting back into my body and running back to the bus after my meditations. One day I narrowly escaped being left behind in the middle of the desert as the bus was taking off for the hotel. As I boarded the bus the tourists shouted at me.

"What the hell were you doing? We have been waiting for you in this stinking hot fucking bus."

Unphased by their insults, I ignored them. I made my way to my seat on the bus avoiding the tourists' angry eyes glaring. Perhaps it was the heat or perhaps the stillness from the meditation. I was enthralled to be in Egypt no matter what the cost. Tour group and all.

Sacred rivers have been a big part of my life. Growing up I loved swimming in rivers and being near any kind of water. The long-awaited five-night Felucca trip scheduled on our tour was suddenly detained by a freak storm, baffling to the locals. That night I set my mind on good weather, and on the following morning we were met with sun and blue skies to set sail.

The iconic Nile River is famed for many thousands of years as no other river. From Lake Victoria she makes her way from the South to North Africa where she meets the Mediterranean Sea. A central life force to the ancient Egyptians, the Nile was responsible for the health of crops and the quick transportation of goods. To this day the storied Nile provides sustenance to modern Egyptians.

Boarding the Felucca, I asked the tour leader about the rooms, so I could accommodate my luggage inside a cabin. He laughed.

"This *is* the cabin, right here! One big cabin for all. We will sleep together under the stars. It is very nice," he assured me.

Others laughed. "There's no champagne service on this boat, love."

I ignored them. I was just surprised. I grew up in Auckland, "The City of Sails." I had been on all kinds of sailing ships, but this was my first on a Felucca. I could sleep under the stars. I had done that many times before. I was on the Nile and nothing else mattered. I could do anything – my dream of being in Egypt had come true and I was the luckiest girl in the world.

And then there was the bathing situation.

The bathing situation was... that the tourists were not bathing. I shower or bathe at least once a day as part of my Yoga lifestyle. A daily cleansing is required in the Yoga sutras to keep a healthy mind, body and spirit. The mind is kept healthy by meditation practices. The spirit is kept healthy by chanting, praying and remembering your soulful dedication. The body is kept healthy by a good diet, exercise, and... bathing.

As enchanting as the Nile is, most in the group were scared to swim in it: crocodiles, germs, disease. With no shower on the boat, my only option was to swim in the Nile: scary to some, but sacred to me.

"Don't do it, you'll catch a disease. You will die. You might pass it on to us. You are crazy. There are microscopic bugs in there." The tourists chimed.

The Nubian boat crew members bathed in the river. They had swum in the Nile their whole lives. They were still alive, so I was not scared. Paying no attention to the naysayers, showing them how I was no "champagne service" woman – and with my mouth closed tight, I dived. The ancient Nile caressed my body. I loved it. Not quite the milky Cleopatra bath, but somehow the water was welcoming. I thought about the cleanliness of the rivers in New Zealand. This water was not clean and downright murky, but I was so happy to be taking my daily ritual bath. I was clean, brave, independent and alive in these famous Nile waters.

At night we slept under the sparkling stars, floating free along the river. It was wondrous, and I drifted off with a contented heart. The sound of the water lapping on the side of the boat. The gentle rocking like that of a baby's cradle. Lulled to sleep by the chirring of night insects on the banks of this historic river. Priceless peaceful perfection. I was grateful, worlds apart and oceans away from New Zealand. An ancient presence embraced me while the whispering winds kissed me goodnight.

To end our tour, we landed in the coastal town of Dahab on the Red Sea before heading back to Cairo. There, I snorkelled amongst the bright coral and colourful fish. Swimming in their underwater world for hours, a mesmerised mermaid, I lost track of all time. In the evenings we shopped at the markets and went to local restaurants full of Shisha[13] smoke dancing through the air and into the night sky.

It was at one of these restaurants, over delicious homemade flat bread and baba ghanoush, that I met Nick, an English man who had been in the area on and off for over 20 years. He knew everyone. He told me about Mount Sinai, and how he had climbed it many times. I was intrigued; Mount Sinai, the sacred mountain where Moses was said to have been given the Ten Commandments.

I was moved by the thought of another adventure and had a deep sense and calling to visit this holy mountain. After rearranging flights to Cairo and hotels, I contacted the guide that Nick had used. We would leave Dahab at 3 am, arrive at the base in a few hours, and ascend in time for sunrise. Though I intended to travel light, Nick urged me to borrow his jacket, though it had been so warm at the Red Sea.

---

13 Hookah pipe used in Arab countries to smoke.

"Just in case." He reassured me.

At the base the day of our ascent, we met the twelve other climbers. Among them was Gary, a loud, chatty English chap, and Yui, a quiet Japanese girl who seemed rather shy. Nick's jacket came in handy right away, as the morning air was chilled and crisp. The morning was still pitch black. The darkness intensified the mystery of this mountain. All I could hear were the steps of my companions, and their breath.

After less than an hour climbing, some climbers lagged behind, already finding the trek challenging. I asked the guide if I could carry on ahead. He instructed those of us in the front to always follow the path.

And then it began to snow.

No one expected this storm. Nick had only warned me of the chill. Just yesterday I was snorkelling off a sunny beach on the Red Sea. And now snow? At first a flurry, the snow quickly strengthened, falling fast and thick and freezing my face and hands. Within what seemed like only minutes, I could not see a metre in front of me, and when I turned around, I saw no one. I had to keep moving while I could still see the path.

The wind screamed. I ignored it and kept climbing, forced forward by the cold.

"Keep going... keep going..." I repeated over and over in my head, a chant in tune with my steps. Then again, the scream on the wind. I stopped for a moment. It wasn't the wind – it was coming from below. I went back down the path towards the cry for help. In the dark, in the blinding snow, I found Gary.

"Please help. Help. Can you help...her..." He was babbling, frantic.

"What happened? Did you hurt yourself? Slow down, it's OK," I assured him.

"She's back there and won't get up. I tried. I can't breathe. I can't feel my fingers. Can you go and help her?"

In the darkness and blinding drifts, I saw Yui on the ground, lying in the snow which had now become a thick blanket on the ground. She was conscious but very weak. I grabbed her and held her up, hoping to share with her what little warmth I had left.

"You must walk, OK? Help me," I said. "Just a few steps and you can stop." I kept reassuring her.

"No, I don't feel good. No good..." Yui's words faded.

My feet and hands frozen, I got us back, step by step, to where Gary waited. We only barely made out the path ahead. It was our only choice. We had to keep going. We formed a chain: I was the middle, with Gary and Yui on either arm. Our shared body heat kept us barely warm. Snot dripped from my nose, tears tumbled down our cheeks, from cold, from fear. The snowstorm was ever increasing, and Yui could not take it any longer.

"No, I will die, I can't...please no." She stumbled and fell again into the snow. I picked her up. I recognized we were all at a breaking point. We could sit in the snow and wait to freeze or keep moving on as best we could. My strength was wavering, but I felt great responsibility to help my companions. We would not give up. Just moments later, as we trudged through the relentless snow, like a mirage in the distance I saw a small shed off the side of the path, lit from inside. Smoke drifted through a small chimney.

Leaving Gary and Yui to keep each other warm, I rustled enough energy to run to the shed. A small Arab man opened the door at my knock, smiling, though he appeared to have been awakened.

"You will help, OK?" I said and, not waiting for a response, I rushed back to collect my friends, so we could all revive some from the warmth of that cabin.

Arm in arm, Gary, Yui, and I made our way to the shed, where a small fire flickered. Our just-roused host showed unquestioning hospitality. He sat us next to the fire and gave us cosy blankets. When we thawed some, we joked about the incongruity of altitude: we were hot at sea level just yesterday and today in a full snowstorm. Our host offered us hot coffee, the most relished relief.

I don't know how long we spent in his little shed home, but when we warmed enough, it was time for us to keep going. We had to continue our pilgrimage to the summit. I thought about the many pilgrims who had been here before us, in worse conditions. I was convinced we would be safe on God's Mountain. I prayed for help, for our final stretch. With this little break, we would have to be refreshed enough to go on.

Thanking our host, we left a donation and set off into the snowstorm once again, now with energy renewed by kindness and coffee. The snow eased as we neared the summit. Day was beginning to break. As the sun touched our faces, a sense of great contentment touched me. What a blessing to greet this day. The snowstorm had passed, we were alive, and closer to God.

The sun rose.

The rest of the group arrived, exhaustion painting their faces, while Yui, Gary and I shined with a sparkling peace. We had bonded through what felt like a near-death experience on the side of the mountain that day. We had overcome this exceedingly rare snowstorm, this test. We had worked through great adversity to reach the summit. God had answered our prayers and kept us safe.

A small church sits at the top of the summit, a painting of Jesus rests at the apex on the outside of the Church. He seemed to welcome us all to God´s safety, there was nothing to fear now. We had survived another day. The church was closed, so I sat down on the front steps to pray and meditate, grateful to be alive, thankful we had all made it and were now safe and welcomed atop Mount Sinai, the holy mountain.

I was not brought up within any specific religious practices. Māori believe in a divine masculine and feminine, and the variety of Gods and Goddesses that live within nature. Buddhism has a formless divinity and follows a path to becoming self-enlightened in this lifetime. Taoists also believe in divinity and the power of nature, and the cultivation of these energies within oneself towards the goal of immortality. In ancient Egypt, a variety of Gods and Goddesses represent the divine, like the Hindu Vedic traditions.

My spirituality has not been limited to one belief. Rather, I have sought the underlying oneness in the ancient traditions, noting the similarities more than the differences. For me, the beauty of spirituality in this modern time is leaning toward unity and diversity, with love at the centre. Love is the greatest power on this planet. I think the word *God* holds many people back from connecting with their own spirituality. For me, *God* is a daily practice of love and offerings; the ultimate relationship one can cultivate.

In our acts of service to save each other that day, we were close to love. We were all so close to God on that journey up Mount Sinai, protected and blessed. I remembered Moses and wondered how he felt when he was on this mountain.

I made my way back to Cairo after my month-long adventure in Egypt. I visited the Pyramids of Giza one last time. As I sat meditating on the pyramid stones, I reflected on my trip in Egypt and the variety of experiences I had. I looked out at the pyramids and saw lines of energy, light grey pencil markings in the sky and space around me. Geometrical shapes and energy around people have been visible to me all my life.

For the first time in my life, I saw straight energy lines running vertical and horizontal. Coming to a perfect stillness in a grid, lining up at the pyramids. I closed my eyes, blinking. The lines have always moved up to down, but this time the lines paused right up against the pyramids, intersecting perfectly, punctuating the feeling of stillness and mystery floating in the air. A divine order.

During my time in Egypt, I noticed a profound shift inside of me, and I was left with a deep sense of my life purpose. I was grateful to have stood in the ancient lands of Egypt, and I was ready to return to the West: renewed, reintegrated and ready for the next phase of life, with deepened inspiration to share for my next Yoga classes.

My final night in Cairo I had a nightmare. I dreamt that my mother called, distressed because my sister was missing. She was crying, I was crying.

"She is gone," she said over and over.

"Your sister, she is gone."

Healing Tao and China

Mantak Chia is an internationally famous Taoist Tantra teacher. Every year he hosts the Healing Tao Retreat in upstate New York. Invited by a Taoist friend from New Zealand, I booked my flights and prepared for one month of back-to-back workshops led by Mantak Chia and some of his top teachers in the West, to widen my spiritual practice with a focus on the ancient Chinese Taoist ways. Tai Chi and Qi Gong are some of the well-known forms.

There, I met teachers who would become dear friends. Joyce Gayheart[14] was a graceful, gentle, feminine embodiment of love and kindness, pure love and sweetness. Her speech made me feel all warm and fuzzy. Her deep blue eyes inspired wonderment in my heart.

In one of her workshops for women only, we centred on healing the divine feminine inside each of us. We meditated on forgiving ourselves and healing the sacred female areas of the body. It was empowering to direct kindness towards places where so many women hold shame, trauma and hurt.

Joyce spoke about the power of the menstrual cycle. The power to heal. That women hold between their legs the power of creation and the greatest pleasure and nectar of life. How we can tap into

14 The former wife of Taoist author and teacher Michael Winn.

incredible creative power within ourselves, opening to our innate intuition and power as women.

My childhood home was full of women whose power was sapped by one man. I never felt good enough; being a woman was more of a curse than a blessing. Laying down and with our eyes closed, Joyce guided us through a meditation. Tears welled up, but I wanted to hold back. I was strong, not vulnerable. I would not cry in front of strangers.

Then I heard other women weeping and I got the permission I needed. I released my tears, too. I let go, I let it all go. Once I started crying, I didn't stop, and the tears flowed incessantly, like a river that had been dammed up far too long.

The room filled with sounds of laughing, crying, whimpering, screaming. I cried for my mother and her mother's mothers, grandmothers and their mothers, for my sisters, for my friends, for all the women in the room, and then for all the women on the planet. This was liberating – crying and laughing together, no holding back, no judgement.

This was one of the most impactful female healings I had done. At the end of the workshop, we were weary and in a daze. I was one of the few who remained sitting while everyone else had left the room. I did not want to move. I did not want to leave the session. I did not want to ever leave the safety of this women's circle. I remained glued to my spot.

Joyce came to me and put her hands on mine. I opened my eyes, and we connected. I do not know how long we stared at each other. I had never held such eye contact with anyone in my life. Her gaze penetrated deep into my soul, and I felt as if I was being seen for the first time. I could see myself for the first time. I was a woman, and proud of it. Strong and vulnerable.

The love I experienced produced a profound shift in my awareness. The safety and compassion were immense. Joyce held my hand through it all. I saw many faces in hers while her eyes remained the same. I had never been so safe and so held. Held in the arms of the

Divine Mother. Held with no judgement, with such love, compassion, kindness. Held in my healing space.

I felt true love and acceptance of myself and all my sisters. We embraced and no words were necessary. The goal of tantra is to be liberated while in the body, liberated through loving kindness. The deepest levels of my mind, body, and soul were raw, vulnerable, radical and free. I was in a state of pure, pampered loving awareness. I had released so much self-doubt and shame in connection to my womanhood in those moments. I was on my path toward empowerment.

That night the sky was filled with exploding bright diamond-like stars. The night insects were resounding across the valley of upstate New York and the air was warm and peaceful. Contentment filled my heart. After the day of emotional waves and purification, I sank into an outdoor Jacuzzi up to my ears and gazed up to the stars, processing all that had taken place personally and collectively.

I was glad to be alone. Thinking about my ancestors who had gone before me. The women and lifetimes of pain and healing. I was feeling safe yet vulnerable in this warm Jacuzzi womb.

As I was lost in peaceful contemplation, an American attending the retreat rumbled into the tub, startling me.

"Good evening, great night huh? Wow, look at the stars!" She spoke in an angular American accent, and my hope for a quiet evening stargazing was suddenly punctured.

"I´m KC Jeronimo, you can call me KC. So how long are you here? Don't you just love it here?" She was peppy and over-eager. Our energies did not match after my day of emotional release.

"Hmm, yeah it's really nice here." I said, closing my eyes, trying to slip back to my inner contemplations.

She was not discouraged and kept up the banter, even peppier. People have said back home that I was loud and outspoken, but in America, it seemed like I was the quiet person.

"So how long have you been here? I'm curious, where are you from?" She was pushing me to engage, and I couldn't ignore her, much as I wanted to. I forced a smile. She was, after all, a woman like those with whom I had just shared a day of deep connection.

"I am from New Zealand. Well, I was born in Australia. My parents were born in New Zealand. But we are mixed with many different blood lines." I spoke.

"What, really? Wow. Are you Māori?" She exclaimed like an excited puppy.

"Yes, well, my father is part Māori, which makes me Māori."

"Oh my *God!* Well, we also have family in New Zealand. Isn't that a coincidence! Well, we are Jewish but we have Māori family there, too. Oh wow! How exciting! We could be related!" This inconceivably strange flight of fancy bubbled from her like a fairy tale.

"Hmm. Yeah, maybe." I said, uninspired by her whimsical musings on our ancestry.

She insisted that we meet again the following night back in the Jacuzzi. I agreed just to put an end to this conversation. I bid her farewell for the night and sought the quiet of my room.

The next evening, I slipped out to the Jacuzzi a little later than the night before, in the hope that KC "Māori roots" would not be there. Spy like, I popped my head over the fence to scope out the scene. The coast was clear. A sigh of relief, and I slinked down into the warm bubbling water again to enter my contemplative space. Just then her familiar voice squealed annoyingly.

"Oh, *there* you are. I am so glad I found you! You won't believe what I have found!" KC said excitedly, holding some sort of book.

"What?" I hoped she didn't see me roll my eyes.

"Well, like I was saying last night, a couple years ago some of my family went to New Zealand for a reunion. To connect with some of our Māori/Jewish family living there, you know? You are Māori and Jewish too, right?"

We hadn't talked about my Jewish roots. My great great great grandfather was a man called Asher Asher, a Jewish man who came to New Zealand from London, back in the 1900s I guessed.

"Yeah, I think so." I said, still unsure what she had up her sleeve.

She handed me her family reunion book. She was so excited that she forgot I was in the Jacuzzi all wet. I wiped my hands on a towel nearby and now I was intrigued. Then she slipped into the warm Jacuzzi alongside me.

On the front cover of her reunion book was *Asher/Keesing Reunion.* How much coincidence was this? My maiden surname is Asher, but she didn't know that. I scanned through a few pages and read "Asher Asher" on one of the family tree lines. I was astounded. KC Jeronimo, the first Jewish woman I had ever met, in the middle of upstate New York – was family?

"So what do you think? Are we connected somehow? We're family?" Her enthusiasm no longer seemed out of place.

"Yes, strange as it seems, we *are* related. This man is my great great great grandfather, Asher Asher," I smiled pointing to the family tree.

"Wow, I knew it as soon as I met you. We *are* family." She squealed.

"Amazing, it is really amazing." I smiled.

In a hot tub in the mountains of upstate New York, we found each other.

"So are you also doing the Healing Tao retreat?" I hadn't seen her in our sessions.

"No no!" she giggled. I am the owner of the retreat."

We spoke for hours about life and our ancestors. About how Jack Asher, my great grandfather, had been quite the lady's man in my tribal lands. Jack Asher had been enjoying the company of many of the exotic and interesting Māori tribal women along the beautiful lake front of Taupo. One lady was my great grandmother Te Arahori Manunui.

KC enjoyed every moment of the ancestral gossip around sordid affairs. Not to mention now that I was *family* she said if there was anything I wanted to be cooked for me special, she would arrange it with the chef. She would happily have the chef prepare 'extras' for me every day. Anything at all.

"Anything?" My mouth watered at the thought of ... dessert.

Up until then the retreat organisers arranged not to serve any desserts during the healing Tao retreats, other than fruit as a sweet to help people stay healthy during their stay and purify the senses. But KC showed me a path to the inner kitchen where I was welcome all hours of the day and night. I was in sugar burst heaven. We agreed that no one should know that all these brownies, cookies, and cakes would be just for *me!* My inner path to enlightenment may still be just out of reach but my path to the inner kitchen was well within my arm's length so I decided to have my cake and eat it.

The same Taoist group that I had studied with in upstate New York was planning a trip to China. I jumped at this opportunity to study with Masters of the original Taoist traditions of China. I knew that I must be a part of this. Not knowing any of the plans I signed up and 7 months later we had landed in China.

The Chinese capital of Beijing evoked memories of Thailand for me: the ancient morphed to modern, bustling streets and ornate temples. The air, a mixture of pollution and moisture, was mysterious and familiar.

One early morning our Taoist group made our way to a local park close to the Temple of Dawn, an imperial temple complex that was used in ancient times by the Ming and Qing dynasties to worship and honour the Heavens on Earth. It was still very crisp and cool, and darkness covered us. Our breaths fogged the morning light.

We removed our shoes and gathered barefoot on the cold, mushy, dewdropped grass. The first soothing songs of birds awakening resounded through the park. Twelve of us began our Qi Gong practice. With effortless flow we synchronised in graceful rhythm. I surrendered to the peace of the moment. Qi Gong and Tai Chi are very gentle yet powerful practices, unlike some Yoga which can be strong and fierce. I found a soothing balance in the flow of these Taoist practises after the many years of strict Yoga practices.

As we were absorbed in our practice, more local people walked by. Some stopped to stare, and others rushed straight past to get to their jobs. What surprised me most were the older people, who came quite close to us and yelled. Some spat at us. I was shocked. Why were they angry with us? Later that day I questioned our leader, who told us that some communist Chinese despise the ancient Chinese practices. I was confused: Why would they react so strongly? Why so much anger? Though I couldn't understand, I had great compassion for them. The Māori people, through a variety of outsiders' influences, had lost some of their ancient wisdom. Some of the Chinese people's own ancient wisdom practices had been lost to them, too, while Westerners outside of China were interpreting those practices in their own way. We all looked for our way to peace.

After the practice, we walked into the main attraction, the Temple of Dawn. The architecture of this sacred temple stood in all its ancient beauty, a true embodiment of Heaven on Earth. Although it had been constructed in 1406, it was kept in sparkling condition, not one tile out of place. We wandered around the temple complex, then I set off on my own.

I could not help but dream about the ancient times, when the emperor and his entourage would have made their grand ceremonies and parades here, in elaborate colourful silk robes with flags and music resounding. I could envision the power and excitement that people must have felt upon entering such a sacred ceremonial space. I sat in a quiet spot for meditation and in a flash, I was absorbed into a trance. The energy here was very strong. We were lucky to be practising the ancient Chinese way here, in the birthplace of Taoism. The blessings of this sacred place fell upon my shoulders, and I was grateful.

Just outside the gates and across the road from the Forbidden City is Tiananmen Square, famous since 1989 as a symbol of rebellion. In that year, a group of students led protests calling for democracy, free speech, and freedom of the press in Communist China. At the peak of the demonstrations sometimes called 'The

'89 Democracy Movement,' up to one million people were present. The protests ended after several months in what became known as the Tiananmen Square Massacre, when troops with assault rifles and tanks fired at the demonstrators.

Estimates of the death toll varied from several hundred to several thousand, with thousands more wounded. Standing in this empty courtyard of Tiananmen Square, our Taoist group spent a moment of silence together, remembering those brave warriors who were fighting for freedoms we take for granted. Standing in this mourning place situated next to one of the most famous and grand palace complexes of ancient China, strange waves of emotion and rebellion stirred in me.

Built in the same era as the Temple of Dawn, the Forbidden City covers over 180 acres of land and consists of 980 buildings. As I walked into the main courtyard, I was in awe of the magnitude and imposing authority of this imperial palace. The carved gilded lions were as ferocious as they must have been six centuries ago, guarding the entrance to the inner palace.

Long ago in the time of the Ming and Qing Dynasties, only the royal family and their employees would be allowed to enter this magnificent palace. It was kept mysterious to the common man and woman. As I walked through one grand courtyard to the next, the palace seemed to go on into infinity through endless halls and gateways. Heaven on Earth. A great surge of excitement swirled in me.

The name *Forbidden City* breathes restriction and formality. I have no idea what came over me – perhaps I had absorbed some of the rebellious spirit from the freedom fighters at Tiananmen Square – but suddenly I was like a tiger released from its cage. Releasing unstoppable energy that had been building, I ran free through the complex. People looked at me with judgement and disdain and I ignored them, running into room after room like a whirlwind. This force was unstoppable, I danced through little alleyways and spun around the sides of this incredible palace, into the luscious green gardens, where I stopped to take in the fresh air and breathe.

I ran with my wild child and felt a great sense of relief. The city forbidden to so many for so long, the city rich with history, had become my playground for those few hours. I was immersed in thoughts of consorts and concubines and all the colours and adornments – and their golden cages.

It was a gruelling process to become one of the chosen girls for the emperor's harem. Candidates passed through many tests of health, beauty and intelligence. It was a great honour for any family if their daughter was chosen, though they would never see or hear from her again. Great pride came from having a daughter who had been chosen. For the daughter it meant a life of the finest clothes and material comforts–any girl's dream. Yet she would face a life of loneliness and bitter rivalry with the many chosen women within the impenetrable perfumed palace walls.

Yes, there were flowing silk gowns of regal colours and designs. Yes, there were distinctive rare adornments draping their necks and earlobes. Their hair and makeup were perfect like porcelain dolls, and they moved with the grace of a swan. Yet unfulfilled desires stirred their fragile hearts. A watchful discerning eye was always close. They were trapped in golden cages, limited to certain areas of the emperor's harem, and never given a chance to roam free in the extensive palace complex. They were never to be seen in their finest beyond the cold stone walls.

Now, I was dancing and running free for all of these women. With every step I felt as if I danced away their restricted past, helped lift their memory from forbidden past to freedom.

The Great Wall of China wrapped its way through the valleys and mountains like the body of a huge grey stone snake. We had arrived early and there were only a few locals wandering. Our Taoist group walked along the Great Wall of China in silence. I, like so many who visit here, contemplated the blood, sweat, and tears it would have taken to construct this massive feat of engineering brilliance.

It was time for our morning Qi Gong practice. We lined up along the ancient wall, in perfect unison, moving and breathing to ancient airwaves. We surrendered to the moment, tuning in to the powerful natural forces around us. What I loved most about these ancient Taoist practices was the honour and reverence toward the natural world. Taoist spiritual practises harmonised sweetly with ancient Māori practises.

> *"I am as strong as the mountain, as soft as the wind. As powerful as the raging rivers and oceans. I am infinite and unbounded like space."*
>
> *- unknown Taoist poet*

Unlike the disgust we witnessed from passers-by in the park at the Temple of Dawn in Beijing, here we were regarded without anger and fury. Twelve westerners practising ancient Taoist arts in peaceful harmony seemed to inspire more respect; it was a heart opening moment, before the days of smartphone cameras; no crowds of people snapping pictures or sneaking videos.

This was captured in universal real time, and the connections felt were timeless. The Qi Gong practice flowed into a stream of consciousness for the practitioners and the viewers: a grace-filled spiritual moment. Energy of golden sunlight circulated in and all around us. The collective mind was quiet and we were moving and breathing as one.

> *"Life is a series of natural and spontaneous changes. Don't resist them, that only creates sorrow. Let reality be reality. Let things flow naturally forward in whatever way they like."*
>
> *- Lao Tzu – Ancient Chinese philosopher and writer*

We arrived at the foothills of Mount Washan. In its belly were caves, thousands of years old, once retreats for Taoist monks. I was excited to be staying three nights alone in one of these caves, fasting except for dry fruit, nuts, and water; a silent retreat. No speaking, though I was looking forward to sharing my chants alone with the wind and the birds. I could hardly sleep that night, imagining with excitement, how this adventure would begin.

I bounced off to the last breakfast I would have for the next three days. With a small bag each we began our ascent into the Mount Washan mountains. Imposing granite towered out of the mist, inspiration for so many scenes from Chinese brush and ink paintings. Nature's fresh air and soft breezes kissed my face. A sense of wonderment filled the air. This mountain is one of the five sacred mountains in the area with a history of ancient religious significance, long home to Taoist practitioners.

Kou Qianzhi, founder of the Northern Celestial Masters, received spiritual revelations here. His influence at the time led the Northern Wei Dynasty to accept Taoism as their official religion. Our leader had said that this was where many Taoist Masters lived, here in this precise mountain range.

Hours passed as we climbed higher and higher. With a bird's eye view we took in the luscious green trees blanketing the misty mountains. After hours of trekking upwards, we took a path off to the side of the trail and began a very steep incline. We were close now. Up still a little higher, we came to a clearing, the access marked by a pathway lined with yellow flags.

The path led us to a massive granite cave with a small entrance carved into the rock. Vegetable gardens and flowers in cultivated patches surrounded this cave. We turned towards an old monk who greeted us with folded hands. We had arrived at the Taoist cave retreat.

He led each of us to the individual cave where we would spend the next three days in solitude. We were told that a gong would sound on the fourth day, and we would make our way back to the main temple cave. I could not wait to be alone in nature.

My cave seemed far enough away in the trees on the mountainside. This would be perfect. I gazed out over rolling hills and became an eagle perched high in my nest.

The sun was getting low and I retreated inside my cave to take a look. It was large, carved by hand thousands of years ago. I imagined the ancient Taoist practitioners and contemplated how they would have thought and felt. I started my own Taoist Qi Gong practice, moving and breathing like the trees, solid as the granite mountains beneath my feet. I had come home.

Alone in the nature of New Zealand growing up, I discovered my first place of worship. Nature was always a safe place for me and my sisters, our temple sanctuary in tumultuous times. From just outside my cave, as the sun was setting far off behind the great mountains, I thought of many people, friends and family. I cried from gratitude for every experience that had led me here to this moment. For the first time in my life, I was truly at peace.

Darkness fell like a thick blanket, and I retired to my cave to sleep. It had been a very long day of hiking through the mountains. I snuggled in safe and ready to try out my new rock bed, a long-carved granite slab along one side of the cave. The back of the cave was like an altar, perfect as a meditation spot. I mapped out my new home, and lay down in a thin travel sleeping bag, smiling. Though this was not the most comfortable bed I had ever slept on, in that moment it was my perfect piece of peaceful paradise.

As darkness engulfed my cave, I called to mind again the ancient practitioners who once lived here. Who were the monks who had carved these caves with such care from the bedrock? How did they practice? As if summoned by my questions, immense energy raced in and all around me. The golden lights I knew as a child entered the cave with me, stronger and more intense than I had ever experienced. Bright, golden energy globes scanned up and down my body, making my whole-body buzz. Out, and in again they flew.

Kundalini, chi, prana, universal energy, divine light. So many names for the same source of "all that is." This special energy had come to me. The intensity of the experience became strong in my spine and head. I focused on breathing and circulating all this chi[15] energy as we were taught in the Taoist Tantric practises. The microcosmic and macrocosmic energy flow connected the energy circuits within my body with the cosmic energy around me.

But this energy was moving too fast, I could not keep up.

I have no idea how many hours this went on, but my exhaustion from the day was replaced by a feeling of acute awareness, a sense of one-ness with everything that came with this energy. I was aware of my body yet possessed by an expansive feeling, as if my body had grown to the size of the cave. I was comforted by these lights I knew as a child, yet worried that I could not handle the intensity.

The energy became harder for me to bear, and I wished it would diminish. I thought that I may not be ready for this intensity, for this long a period. Adventurous as I was, daring as I was – I was a young girl just beginning on my spiritual path. The Taoist practitioners before me who lived in these caves had lifetimes dedicated to these arts. They could wield the power of the winds and rain. I could barely wield my own thoughts, let alone this universal power. I kept breathing through.

Gradually the energy subsided, and it became the familiar golden energy, more comforting than challenging, softer with the touch of an angel. The golden light swirled, funnelling smaller, then larger – leading into an array of colourful mandalas. I knew, then, that I was safe and protected, and in peaceful exhaustion I drifted off into dream-filled sleep.

The days in the cave were spent meditating, doing Qi Gong and contemplating. This was the first time in my life I had spent such

15 Chinese word for vital life force energy; same as Prana in Sanskrit.

a long time alone in nature. Unique as it was, it became natural and healing to me, as I encountered a deep peace both inside and around me, quieting my distracting thoughts.

I was alone but not lonely within the freedom and space. I wept, I sang songs in Māori that expressed connection to the wind and how it cleanses us. I sang to the trees and gave honour and thanks to the sun. To be with oneself is a special opportunity for self-healing and contemplation.

The hunger came on the second day, after eating only dried fruits and nuts. The feeling in my stomach reminded me of when I was a small girl and each year, my sisters and I took part in a 40-hour "famine." We requested donations from family and friends, and the proceeds were given to a charity in Africa that fed people experiencing real famine.

Here in the cave, I knew that four days was far from a famine. I knew now that I could shift my awareness to something else, a training I wasn't yet aware of as a child. The power of the mind can be one's greatest friend or greatest enemy. I dived deeper into Qi Gong practice and meditated even more. On the third day, my hunger was gone.

I still missed a nice warm shower, but I had managed the hunger. My tongue desired only what it was given, and the smallest morsel of dried fruit and nuts inspired a meditation on appreciation.

I found my senses more alive. My ears sharp, I tuned into the concert of birds throughout the mountain valley. My eyes became aware of so many shades and textures of green, illuminated by a sparkling sun. Everything had a pulsating energy that drew warm arms around me. The mountains had become my friends. The trees, my parents. The sun and clouds, my messengers, and the breeze, my caring companion.

I didn't go to the cave with a specific plan, I simply wanted to get closer to the way of the Taoist monks. I spent only three days – I wasn't meant to be an ascetic. Yet the nature around me during those three days, the solitude, the connection with a peaceful, contemplative space away from the distractions of daily life allowed me to rest for a moment in the divine embrace. Emerging, everything looked bright, and I found that I kept the cave with me in my heart. Not the dark, foreboding cave of metaphor – but this, a sanctuary, a sacred inner space, untouched, and available to me any time I would need it.

Lao Tzu was an ancient Chinese philosopher and writer, the reputed author of the *Tao Te Ching*[16], the founder of philosophical Taoism, and a deity in religious Taoism and traditional Chinese religions. He formed 'The Way of Celestial Masters,' the first organised religious Taoist sect in history.

In later Taoist tradition, Lao Tzu came to be seen as a personification of the Tao. He is said to have undergone numerous *transformations* and taken on various guises and various incarnations throughout history to initiate the faithful in the Way, the Tao. Religious Taoism often says that the 'Old Master' did not disappear after writing the Tao Te Ching, but rather spent his life immortal, travelling and revealing the Tao to others.

We stayed in the village where he was reputed to be born, in an old temple turned hotel. Exploring the village, I came across another old temple that invited my curiosity. It seemed to be unoccupied, though it was in good condition, and I assumed it must be tended by someone. I wanted to investigate and climbed inside and to an upper terrace that allowed a view of the bamboo forest surrounding us.

Enjoying the silence and solitude of this peaceful space, I began to practise Qi Gong, breathing in the crisp countryside air, punctuated by a rich incense. Calmed and content after my practise, I made my way back down the stairs into the main temple sanctuary.

16 Ancient Chinese book of wisdom.

I stood admiring the altar and beautiful decorations, inscribed red and yellow flags gently swaying in the wind, carved wooden columns, and the shining roof tiles adorning the temple.

As I turned to leave, I was startled by a small man who seemed to emerge suddenly from the shadows without a sound.

Had he been watching me the whole time? Was this the main caretaker of the temple?

I greeted him with hands folded in respect in the Taoist way and said *hello* in the simple Chinese I had learned during my trip.

He smiled and invited me to follow him to a small courtyard, where he offered me tea. I could tell he was a monk by the way he was dressed, in pure white robes. As we sipped green tea, I signalled and smiled, best I could, about the beauty I had found in his temple. He smiled, then to my surprise he pulled out a wrinkled map of the world. He pointed to himself and then China on the map. When he pointed to me, I showed him New Zealand, and he looked puzzled. Perhaps no one had ever come to visit his temple from New Zealand before?

He tucked his map back under his robe, leaving the question between us, and stood to re-enact some of the Qi Gong sequence that I had done on his temple rooftop. Embarrassed, I could feel my cheeks burning red. It appeared he had been watching me. He smiled then motioned to himself and said something I couldn't understand. He paused, eyes closed, and for some time stood very still. Then he bowed as every monk warrior does to begin. He took a deep breath in.

The warrior monk began to flow. He moved with precision, each breath on purpose and every movement sinuous as a cobra. I had never seen anyone practise like this. I was enamoured by his skill. His concentration was crystalline. I was in the presence of a true warrior monk. Not one movement out of place. I tried not to blink, spellbound. His divine dance was potent as a lion, graceful as a swan. As he moved through his flowing form, his pace quickened, swifter with each pounce. Still no hand or foot out of place. His entire being emanated the warrior spirit of old.

All ancient monks trained in martial arts. The Qi Gong and forms of Taoism have roots far back to the time of the true warriors. They knew the importance of a steady mind through meditation and preparation, with a balanced emotional, mental, physical, and spiritual state.

> *"The best warrior leads without haste, fights without anger, overcomes without confrontation. He puts himself below and brings out the highest in his men. This is the virtue of not confronting, of working with the abilities you have, of complying with the laws of Heaven. This is the ancient path that leads to perfection."*
>
> *- Lao Tzu, Tao Te Ching*

This warrior monk could fell an enemy in one move. This man was not doing the form, the form was doing him. We were suspended in time, the bamboo groves swaying in perfect harmony. A golden light energy warmed my body. I was in the presence of greatness.

Coming to a close, the monk ended with his hands in honour at his heart and bowed. All great teachers I have met in this world, bow and honour something much greater than themselves. He turned to me, back to his friendly form. I could only express myself in tears, no words could express what grace he had just shared, even if I could speak his language. We smiled at one another, and in great honour and respect I bowed to the true warrior monk in front of me.

I left him, yearning to learn more from him, though realising I wasn't likely to see him again. Yet that night he appeared in my dreams. He led the way on a wild, wonderful journey into a lucid dreaming space. A new-found paradise. We danced a battle with one another. Flying over rooftops, a stride became a leap and then we were flying effortlessly over bamboo trees and mountains amidst boundless beauty. We soared to bright sunlit heights, dancing with the wind, flying with the birds and the bees. It was a warrior love dance, exhilarating and ecstatic, set against a night sky full of shooting stars.

I woke up amazed at this lucid dreaming experience. I had found a teacher – or perhaps he found me. When he came to me in dreams, I knew that he would continue to teach me. They say when the student is ready, the teacher appears. Even if it was only for a few hours, this teacher activated me through the dream space and the transmission was alive within me. It takes great dedication and discipline to master these ancient practices. I wanted to become solid and grounded like this true warrior monk. I wanted the unshakeable concentration that this true warrior monk embodied. Even if I could not master these practices as he had done, he inspired that dedication and discipline in me.

Tibetan pilgrimage

AS PART OF THE TAOIST trip to China there was a wonderful side trip planned to Tibet. On a small aeroplane from China to the sacred lands of Tibet, we were welcomed by the snow-peaked mountains of the towering Himalayas. Our faces squished against the windows to catch a glimpse through the blanket of clouds, we wept, touched to the core by the sheer natural beauty and strength of these famed mountains.

We had landed in Tibet. As we drove away from the airport, we stopped the car along the roadside to sit on the banks of the river. I did a short traditional Māori prayer and soon the others in the group had also stopped their cars. In awe and amazement, we sat together on the side of the road which hugged this river valley, admiring the Tibetan landscape and beauty. We began our Qi Gong practice of cultivating *chi*, breathing in the beauty deep inside, exhaling gratitude all around us. Invigorating and inspiring, the most loving welcoming to the lands of Tibet.

Temple of Mother Nature

Into a divine space
Time passes without a trace
Sacred waters of old flow
Branches of mystic trees hang low

Compassionate hearts embrace
Grace imbued nectar taste
A messenger of God sits next to me
In a moment I was set free
A magic forest revealed
Deeper truth concealed
Golden starlight bath
Further along the blessed path
Healing waterfalls
Lovers singing calls
Drunk on natures bliss
Savouring a beloved kiss

One morning in Lhasa, I woke up early and walked to the Jokhang temple. It was still dark as the sun had not quite come up. The streets were still, a contrast from the normal crowds of monks and pilgrims that swarm the area in daytime hours. I heard an enchanting woman's voice singing in the distance. As I got closer to the temple, I saw a woman chanting the holy Tibetan Buddhist compassion Mantra *Om Mani Padme Hum.*

She was half my size, almost the size of a child. She was prostrating to the ground, lying with her full body in offering, then raising her arms towards the sky and again down to the ground. On and on she chanted and prostrated. Just out of view, I watched in awe, her pure mind-body-soul prayer mesmerising.

Though she seemed ancient, her stamina and strength reflected the energy of a twenty-year-old. She paused for a moment and turned around and caught my eye. Embarrassed at being caught watching her, I wondered if she would be annoyed, but I didn't break eye contact as she exuded such a loving warmth. She invited me to join her. As we chanted and prostrated together, I again filled with the familiar warm, golden energy, an energy that filled me but moved past the borders of my own body.

> *"Om Mani Padme Hum..Om Mani Padme Hum...Om Mani Padme Hum...Om Mani Padme Hum."*

We were in a tantalising trance together. I could feel her eyes on me, and when I looked at her, tears flowed down her cheeks, a river of kindness. I could feel the genuine compassion, and deep humility circulating directly between our hearts. The mantra continued as tears flowed around her smile. She seemed to have accepted me, a total stranger, as a dear friend, trusting me and including me in her special morning prayer.

I was familiar with chants, and I knew they were powerful. When I first started chanting this mantra in New Zealand, it brought me to a space of inner peace within a few minutes. It was a natural and freeing way for me to express the language of my soul, pure and potent. Chanting unlocked a deeper part of myself that wanted a voice to share the love that came into my heart when I sang. My authentic voice, sung, shared and heard. As now, in this sacred corner of Tibet.

All barriers dissolved and all that was left was the mantra of compassion holding us in this unforgettable moment. Time passed without notice, and as the sun rose, people began gathering. She stopped when she knew it was time, and gave me a big hug, smiling at me with deep brown eyes. I cried folded in her soft embrace, the feelings of compassion and acceptance from her lodged deep inside my mind and heart. A familiar hug, like that of my great grandmother Te Arahori. Just as suddenly as I had come upon her, she vanished into the crowds.

> *"Om Mani Padme Hum...Om Mani Padme Hum...Om Mani Padme Hum...Om Mani Padme Hum."*

This surprising woman was another teacher, appearing for me as I was open and ready to learn. She had no master's degree or certificates of greatness. What she knew was not learnt in any institution.

She embodied the greatest teachings of all: True compassion. The sincerity of the compassion mantra she sang was a priceless gift she gave me. She was compassion personified. When I chant this mantra, I still hear her voice. She lives inside of me now, in my mind's heart, into eternity. This was to be the beginning of a lifelong dedication to these ancient healing chants.

A warrior monk in China, and this enchanted lady in Tibet: I had met, by pure chance, two unconventional wise and authentic teachers. I was finding that, when I ventured beyond my comfort, straying a bit from the well-travelled path into different spaces with an open mind and heart, doors opened, and my teachers appeared to push me on my spiritual quest, to deepen my faith that I was *able* and *deserved* to progress on my spiritual path. These teachers instilled a greater sense of hope, and I felt a duty to them, to follow in their footsteps as best I could.

Pilgrims travel thousands of miles by foot to pay their respects at the Potala Palace. Year-round, thousands of religious pilgrims circle the palace with prayer wheels and beads to request and share blessings. I was excited to purchase my own prayer wheel at the entrance to the Potala Palace, as many pilgrims do. The prayer wheel is a hollow wooden or metal cylinder with a wooden handle. *"Om mani padme hum"* mantra is written thousands of times inside the cylinder on a long piece of paper, rolled up and placed inside the cylinder. This is the mantra of compassion. Each time you spin the prayer wheel, the prayers written inside the cylinder are said to be released and go out to all beings on the planet, many times over.

Off I went spinning the prayer wheel and chanting the compassion mantra. Before we arrived at the entrance to the palace, a group of elder Tibetan pilgrims ushered us in another direction, smiling and encouraging us to follow. Walking beside them, we arrived at a space with rows and rows of giant prayer wheels, mounted into the ground. As pilgrims walked by they set each one to spin.

We followed behind our spontaneous Tibetan guide and did as the other pilgrims, spinning the larger prayer wheels with one hand, and our smaller one with the other. The compassion mantra emanated in all directions. Blessed to be part of this ancient ceremony, I was entranced as we made our way around the parikrama[17] pathway, incense and bells resounding through the air.

Our group was on the lower plane, the palace towering above us as if floating in the clouds. Though my attention was below with the movement of pilgrims, flowing like a river, I could feel the presence of the palace watching over us. After what seemed like a moment but was likely several hours, we had completed the full circuit. The compassion mantra resounded inside of me.

As we at last entered the palace, my familiar light raced golden into my spine and coursed throughout my body. All sound faded. The mantra had taken over. As I looked around the palace, it was familiar. I was intrigued by the rich decorative painting on the walls, the carvings and Buddhist ornamentations. The energy infused here was calm, even though it had been ransacked by the Chinese army years ago. A feeling of safety entered my mind and heart.

This palace had once been the home of the current Dalai Lama, along with many of the Dalai Lama incarnations before him. I was struck by the thought of his sudden escape after the failed Tibetan uprising. In disguise in the middle of the night, he left the palace and arrived on the border of Northern India where he was given safe refuge. I had a deep sense of sadness that the Dalai Lama could not live in his own home in Tibet, this beautiful palace that had been home to all the Dalai Lamas for hundreds of years. I felt a weight in my chest when contemplating his need to escape to save his life.

Walking around the Potala palace I was in a deep trance; I had been chanting the compassion mantra for many hours now and it

17 Clockwise pathway used in Buddhist and Hindu prayer. "Pari" in Sanskrit means "around," "krama" means "progression of events."

had taken me over. My eyes were now only half open and it felt as if I floated around. All the while my prayer wheel was still spinning, and I continued reciting the mantra. For a brief moment I tried to fully open my eyes and see where the others were in my group, yet as soon as I widened my eyes, I felt dizzy. So, I half-closed them again and went back to the mantra inside of me. My internal stillness surrendered me to the trance of the compassion mantra.

I eventually made it to comforting gardens within the palace grounds. The others from the group eventually found me and we continued to walk the gardens. Still completely absorbed, I followed along walking, moving and breathing to the pulse of the compassion mantra.

"Om Mani Padme Hum, Om Mani Padme Hum..."

The Jokhang Temple in Lhasa, built in 652, is considered to be the spiritual heart of the city and the most sacred temple in Tibet. Visiting one morning, I heard a faint background of mystical chanting, an accompanying drum beat I could feel deep in my chest. Drawn toward the sound, I made my way up steep stairs and came to a beautiful ancient wooden carved door.

The chanting was loud now just behind the door. I tried to open the door, but it was stuck. Or locked? No matter – something was pushing me to go towards the music, I leaned against the heavy door and pushed with all my might. Successfully the door opened with a bang, and I let out a sigh.

To my great surprise a crowd of around 50 monks were gathered on the rooftop, and with the thud of the door, the music and chanting suddenly stopped to pin-drop silence. I could feel my cheeks go fire red, prickling my skin and face. I began to sweat. I must be up to my ears in trouble now.

One of the older monks smiled at me. He led me to the group and gave me a place to sit down on a soft, silky cushion, bang smack in the middle of the entire gathering. My heart was thumping so loud, it seemed it would have overpowered their drums. The chanting began again, the music they produced an unusual concert of conch, bells, hand drums, finger symbols, and massive gongs. The mixture of deep tones and tiny tinkling's was hypnotic. I closed my eyes to meditate.

The drumbeat was precise, the chanting buzzing through me. Waves of dreamy sleep started to creep over me. I faded, drifting in and out of consciousness. I tried a Yogic technique of gazing at one thing. I chose a spot on the floor. It only lasted a few seconds and there I was again back in my near slumber. I looked over at the monk who had sat me down, pleading with my eyes.

"Please read my mind: 'What do I do? I'm drifting off."

He smiled and motioned with his head dropping to the side and closing his eyes. Was he giving me permission to lie down? I could not resist any longer, and with the permission I perceived from him, I laid down my weary head, in the middle of the congregation.

When I awakened later, I was covered with a blanket. No one was around. No monks, no instruments. How long had I been sleeping? Wiping the dreams from my eyes, I saw the monk, sitting not too far away, smiling. He spoke in laughter. He motioned for me to stay sitting and went off to get tea.

Grateful for the wake-up tea, I gulped before I even caught a whiff of what I soon learned was every Tibetan's favourite: yak's milk tea. An "acquired taste," it tasted like tea made with very old milk. Rancid milk. Very, very bad old rancid milk. I drank quickly, in politeness, and gratitude for his kindness. He topped me up with more tea every time I was about finished, with true Tibetan hospitality. I finally held my hand over the cup and smiled back at him. My new friend had allowed me into the chanting experience, and graciously gave me a space to rest. Buddha had showered his compassion through this kind monk.

USA and meditation of a lifetime

On return from China and Tibet, I lived in Brooklyn, just over the bridge from New York City, staying with friends and going to dance auditions, trying to land a job to earn money again after being away from work while on pilgrimage in China and Tibet.

My heart was not in the hip-hop dance world, but it paid good money. The money I earned from teaching Yoga was not sufficient for the travelling lifestyle I was living. So with reluctance I caught trains all over New York, running from audition to audition.

One day, exhausted and uninspired with the relentless auditions, I skipped out on the rest of the appointments for the day, lured by the swaying American Elm trees at Central Park in the heart of Manhattan. It was time for a breather.

The July heat trapped in the city was a thick blanket hovering overhead and the oasis of Central Park was a welcome relief. I found a cosy spot under large welcoming trees to lay down.

I was anxious and uncertain what to do. On one hand I had just experienced incredible spiritually opening trips in China and Tibet, meeting inspiring teachers and feeling peace and contentment for the first time in my life. Then on the other hand, I was only two months back in the west and already my sacred inner retreat space was teetering out of balance.

Mini-panic attacks swirled in my unsteady heart, self-doubt and self-judgement sounded loudly inside my head. The engrained 'not good enough' story was taking centre stage. My insecurity was weighing me down, heavily into the ground.

I needed to earn money. Dancing was a way that had helped me pay the bills and fly around the world. Yet the other part of me yearned and burned to devote my life to the Yoga teachings and help people heal. I was essentially living two parallel worlds. One an ego driven hip hop dance world, and the other a true Yogi path. I was confused, I did not know what to do. I was at a crossroads and had no idea which direction to go toward.

As I lay down on the soft grass, I began to pray. I asked God to give me guidance, I was desperate for a sign of what I should do next. Within the confusing unrest, tears came rolling down my cheeks.

"Please God guide me, I need your help, give me a sign of what I should do next. Which path should I take?" I opened my eyes and looked up at the beautiful bright blue sky.

Above me circling in the sky were four eagles, gliding gracefully with ease and synchronicity. I knew immediately this was a *tohu* sign. The Māori give special significance to the eagle. I used to spot them often in New Zealand. It was comforting to feel these eagles circling above me. The panic and insecurity eased away.

I knew God had answered me and given me this sign. I still had no idea what I was supposed to do or what the sign meant. But even just the sight of the eagles lifted the confusion from my heart, and I left the park feeling much lighter, knowing something was about to shift for me, keeping faith in my divine protector.

The shift came through a phone call from a dear friend of mine from New Zealand. He happened to be staying in New York and invited me to the Hamptons later that week, where he would be teaching Yoga workshops. I already had so many auditions lined up, and having skipped some already, my responsibility to find work was tugging at me. I told him 'No.'

When I got off the phone I went for a walk and the questions came. Why did I say 'no'? What was important to me right now? To find a job? Yes. To find peace? Yes. How could I justify going to the

Hamptons to do Yoga workshops with my friend, while abandoning my responsibilities in the city to find work?

Then I remembered the eagle sign....

I called him back. "Can I still come? Is it too late?" I expressed my excitement at the illogical decision I was making.

I had a couple of hours to pack my things and get on a train from Brooklyn to Manhattan. The rush and deadline made the whole thing even more exciting. I ran down the sidewalk to the Hampton jitney bus station. My friend, dressed in white, his long grey hair flowing in the wind, waved out to me. I had made it, in perfect divine timing just minutes before the bus departed New York City, Hamptons bound.

We arrived at East Hampton to a warm welcome by a dear Yogini, Lalita (Kate). She drove us to her home, and we entered by a beautiful tree-lined canopy driveway. Inside the house, kids were running around. I noticed right away pictures of Neem Karoli Baba known by his devotees as Maharaji[18] in every room. My heart bubbled and a feeling of *coming home* washed over me. I was warm and safe here. I had an instant connection to this very cheeky-looking man. I awoke to his picture each morning and he came to me in a dream, as did other Indian teachers I did not know.

Rameshwar Das was Lalita's husband, and one of the official photographers of Maharaji. He had a large collection of photos kept safe in his basement, a treasure trove for him and other Maharaji devotees. Later on, as I got to know the family and he shared some photos with me, tears welled up in his eyes as he recalled divine love-filled experiences with this great saint, his Guru Maharaji.

In this home, I learnt how a healthy community function. Everyone, old and young, helped to prepare amazing vegetarian feasts, cleaning up afterwards, too. We took turns looking after the children – everyone stepped in to lighten the load – unlike in my family home where explosions would be set off in an instant, where

18 Maharaji - means king in Sanskrit, a name used for great Guru's.

my mother scurried ever more frantic and anxious to complete household chores.

I admired how respectfully the family spoke to one another. Even when the children's tantrums would inevitably kick off, non-violent communication and respect characterised these episodes and was heart-warming to witness. I was grateful to be living in a loving environment that I had so longed for growing up.

I originally went to stay in the Hamptons with my Yogi friend for a few days, yet I did not end up leaving for months. Lalita and I became good friends, and I became the Nanny of their two beautiful and cheeky children, James and Mirabai.

One of my favourite things to do was take the children down into their massive colourful beautiful bountiful garden to collect offerings. We called it our secret garden, just far enough away from the main house, covered by beautiful swaying trees and bluebells, with every variety of vegetable you could imagine. I was now a fairy of the forest in East Hampton. Oversized courgettes glistened in the sun under protective leaves. Juicy red tomatoes climbed up carefully placed trellises. Rows and rows of sweet-smelling basil grew tall and proud with the most enchanting aroma. The garden seemed endless in its ability to provide us with nature's gifts. This secret garden was the market for our delicious vegetarian feasts. This home felt very much home.

The many guests who came and went through the Hamptons house stayed a few days or weeks and were always interesting characters. Many had been friends of Ram Dass[19], who had met Maharaji when he was in his body living in Vrindavan and Kainchi, India, in the late 60s.

The story of my spiritual path cannot be complete without including the inimitable Ram Dass and my growth through his inspiration. Ram Dass was a revolutionary spiritual teacher who wrote the famous book on Yoga and meditation, *Be Here Now.* In the sixties

19 Further information on Ram Dass can be found in endnotes.

on return to the US from India after meeting Maharaji, Ram Dass became a teacher of transcendental meditation, writing several spiritual books and holding massive gatherings at his family's huge estate, hosting an array of hippies and seekers of truth and love. *Be Here Now* became one of the most popular new age books of all time.

To be in the presence of Ram Dass was to be in the presence of true love. His personality was soft and gentle, and he was often surrounded by admiring devotees. The first time I met him was at the yearly Bandara festival that Maharaji devotees organise. We were at a friend's countryside home in Massachusetts, filled with people greeting and hugging one another.

All of a sudden the sweet setting changed. People were frantically running around.

"What has happened? Why is everyone running around?" I was curious.

"Ram Dass is here, Ram Dass is coming." A man nearby answered me with great excitement.

Having not yet met Ram Dass, I was still not sure what the fuss was all about, so I headed over to join the crowds. A man in a wheelchair emerged, shaking hands and greeting all with respect and smiles as he made his way through to the barn.

Later, a friend filled me in. Ram Dass was like the grandfather of the Maharaji community. The love and adoration the group bestowed upon him that day was incredible. To be honest, at first I found it all a bit odd, people touching his feet, crying, overwhelmed with emotion.

Seeing people demonstrating this kind of devotion to a man was bewildering to me. I had yet to deepen my experience in India, as Ram Dass had done. I had yet to discover the devotional heart that dwelled inside of me, waiting to love and adore in open expressive ways.

The time spent with the friends of Ram Dass in the Hamptons house, with Ramesh, Lalita and their kids, helped me recognise my devotional heart that had yearned my whole life to be part of a healthy family; how to serve others with genuine care and kindness. I learnt that a healthy community can and does exist. My heart was on fire with love and service thanks to them. I had begun my path of Bhakti.

Ramesh, Lalita and their kids were planning a holiday to India and asked me if I'd like to join them. I could barely contain my excitement. I dreamt of being in an ashram, happily meeting Māori people there. For me the Vedic Indian tradition overlapped heavily with the ancient Māori beliefs. I found them intimately connected, one and the same. They left a few weeks earlier than I, so I stayed with a friend in New York City to get my Indian visa and other bits and pieces sorted for the trip to India. I had been given lists from a variety of friends who had already been to India many times, knowing the few comforts that a westerner travelling to India might need: chocolate, vitamins and especially good herbal remedies for all the little bugs I would pick up along the way.

On the morning of October 10, 2004, just before I was about to leave for India, I experienced the most blissful meditation of my life. I was intrigued to attend a Buddhist class, as I loved to meet new teachers and learn new philosophies and approaches to the one true essence. My heart had already been swayed by the Buddha when I had lived in Thailand. I was still chanting the Buddhist chants that I had learned there and found great peace each time I recited them.

We arrived in a cosy practice space just outside of New York City. Many traditional Buddhist wall hangings adorned the space, full of ancient script. It felt inviting and new to me. The Master led us into a guided meditation, and very quickly I felt myself soaring up and out into the cosmos, through the stars with many colours swirling around me. I felt a deep sense of oneness and felt my spirit flying away into timeless space.

After what I learned later was nearly two hours, the Master gently brought us back and grounded us again into our bodies. I didn't want to leave this gentle yet powerfully expansive state. I was blissful.

Later I would learn that this meditation precisely corresponded with the moment my sister left her physical body.

On the ride back, I was eager to tell my friend about the most blissful meditation I had ever experienced. I had spoken but a few words when suddenly I felt very heavy, very down. A dark cloud hovered over me. I felt as if my head were a stone, impenetrable, dense, dull.

I came down too fast, my friend joked. Like an acid trip, he said, but there was no explanation for such a sudden and violent mood change – meditation is not like acid.

"You have to come down once you've gone up," he smiled.

We laughed and I agreed, just to agree, but deep down my intuition, my gut knew that something was not right. I reflected on my spiritual practice, thinking I had so far to go, that maybe I just couldn't handle the bliss state.

Then I remembered the vulture.

Just a few days before my Buddhist meditation experience, I was with another friend. We were driving in the mountains near Woodstock to a contemplative spot in the woods, one of her favourite places to go.

Suddenly, we nearly ran into a huge black vulture in the middle of the road. It swooped up over our car, its large wings brushing our windows. The car seemed to shake from the force of the giant bird. A dead black snake, the vulture's lunch, was stretched across the road. Feeling the vulture perched in a tree above us, waiting for us to leave, we crept like a snail, avoiding the snake's dead body to avoid further enraging the vulture. As we drove away, I looked back and saw the vulture landing again on its prey, massive and hungry.

My friend claimed that the vulture and snake were a sign. She said something was going to happen, things were going to change. I was certainly shaken by the vulture and snake, but didn´t see how it could mean change, particularly. She offered no further explanation, and I kept that shocking vision of terrible wings in my mind. When she brought it up again later that day, she told me that I was about to have my world shaken up. That I have not known true suffering, and I would know soon. She seemed insistent, angry even.

When I got back to my friend's apartment my email read:

> "*Urgent: Please call home to New Zealand!*"

My sister was missing.

The dream in Egypt… The vulture and the snake…

…Then the I Ching man in China.

He was in the middle of a forest, sitting alone in a path lined with bamboo. I hadn't expected to run across anyone on this solitary path, and initially doubted his motive as he invited me to sit. He had a small mat covered with ancient Chinese symbols of the *I Ching* along with Chinese pendants. The *I Ching* is a divination practice that has existed in China for thousands of years. I gave him a chance. He held my hand and began to read the *I Ching* for me, tearing up, but I couldn't understand.

We rustled up some paper from my handbag and he wrote. I held back my own tears, shaken by his, as I reached into my bag to give him some money. He wouldn't take it, just pushed the paper into my hands.

After dinner that evening, I asked the restaurant manager to look at the note. He translated the script to English, with the expected "You are a very fortunate person. You are healthy and strong." Like any random fortune I have run across. But then he paused.

"Oh, don't believe these people, they only take money and they're no good." He looked annoyed.

I thought that, also – but was proved wrong. I asked the restaurant manager to continue.

"You will go through a very big challenge that will change your life. A death."

I did not want to hear anymore. Was I going to die?

Signs and foretelling, coincidence or not, I was on a plane home to New Zealand, pleading with my sister's picture that she must, please, be OK.

The children of the mist - *Nga tamarki o te kohu*

Te Piha is an iconic black sand beach not far from where I was brought up in West Auckland, on the west coast of New Zealand. The entire west coast seems covered with a glistening black sand, a sparkling blanket. Beautiful, light-filled, captivating -- like my sister. It was here she disappeared. My dolphin-sister, my soul-sister, my best friend. Her name was Iraena Rama Te Awhina. The second part of her name in Māori so aptly means

> *"The one who helps bring the shining light."*

Despite her many struggles with bipolar episodes over the years since we were teenagers, Iraena had shared so much light with me and with the world. Her sweetness lit up every room she entered. I remember this magic when we used to go out dancing together. The joy and light that emanated from her was so powerful, that she could get a listless room up and on their feet within just a few minutes.

Perhaps because she suffered these imbalances, it was challenging for her to remain on the light side of her spirit. She missed it sometimes and was able to grasp more than others the beauty and power of that light. And the terror of the dark.

I sat down with great suspicion when the police investigators arrived on the scene at Piha.

"I need a full brief on what has happened here. Where is my sister?"

"We need to ask you some questions first. We need to know some more information about you, to help us in this investigation."

"About ME? YOU should be doing the talking now. Fill me in first."

I scowled and the enraged warrior in me clenched, but I needed to hear them out.

Piecing together their verbal report from that day, with subsequent tapes that we heard a full month later, the story of Iraena's disappearance unfolded in grim, heart-wrenching detail.

In the early hours of October 11th, 2004, my sister made an emergency call to the police.

"Can someone please come and help me? I am at a friend's place in Piha but I don't feel safe here." I recognized the stress in my sister's voice.

"What exactly is going on?" the police dispatcher asked.

"I don't know. Well, I am not sure...I don't know... maybe my drink has been spiked?" Iraena was clearly quite nervous. "I am being pressured to have sex. I just don't feel safe here." She sighed. "I have just run out of the house; I grabbed this phone on the way out but I don't have anything with me. I don't want to go back there." She was audibly panting, on the run now.

The police held her on the line, increasingly agitated. They seemed to dismiss her need for help, brushing her off, just another young girl looking for a free ride home.

"This is not a helpline. This is the police, so I suggest you call the 0800 number." The policeman snarled at her. "I can send you a taxi which you can pay for, what is the address again?"

The taxi never arrived. The police sent it to the wrong address, on the opposite side of Auckland nowhere near Piha, or so they say.

Piecing together the story through multiple sources as we investigated this tragic lapse, we learned that Iraena was picked up on that stormy night by two women who lived at a local Piha beachfront home. I'm sure she felt initial comfort from women, mothers, and caregivers. They took her to their home, gave her a warm robe, some tea, and a bed to sleep on. Though they noted she seemed "out of it," they did not seek to call anyone who could help her.

Instead, the son of one of the women sat talking with my sister into the early hours of morning. We'll never know what they said. But something spooked Iraena, and suddenly, she rushed out of the house and back into the storm. No one from that house went after her. She was off alone running into her fate-filled night.

The very last people to see my sister were a couple walking their dog at around 2am. They saw Iraena stop under one of the last streetlamps before Lion Rock. She was naked. The dressing gown she was given was found later, near the streetlamp. The couple watched her bow down to kiss the earth, then bow in each of the four directions before she walked purposefully towards the edge of the raging ocean.

Our ocean. The ocean where we had once danced with the dolphins.

She was failed by a system that lacked empathy, by individuals who did not, or would not do enough to help a young girl alone in the middle of a stormy night. Were people judging my beautiful sister? Why are the woes of women not taken seriously? I felt my own failure to help her in the pit of my stomach.

When I learned of Iraena's last moments, I was the picture of agony, my heart ripped from my chest. I could not breathe. I, too, drowned. Our ocean. The ocean where we had once played and dreamed had swallowed her? I was gripped by physical pain unlike anything I had ever experienced, every inch of my body screamed her name. Iraena, my beloved best friend, my sister for whom I was always present. Except this time, I wasn't…The thought of having failed to save her, of losing her forever became my all-too-imaginable torture.

While scrambling for facts around the loss of my sister, I learned that the morning of Iraena's disappearance, a whale had beached itself and was dead in Kare Kare, washed up on the shore next to Piha.

The local *iwi*[20] had prayed for this whale as is custom in Māori tradition. The whale gave its body as a sacrifice. Not only a sacrifice but a deep and profound blessing. Māori have a close relationship with both whales and dolphins.

I was still not ready to believe that I would never see or hold or speak with my sister again, though I could not shake the whale beaching as yet another ominous sign. Search and rescue teams swarmed the rural coastlands, searching for a dead body. My sister's body. My remaining sisters and I conducted our own searches, looking everywhere, sometimes driven by fake leads from prank callers.

The fire of separation from my sister and the cloud that engulfed my family home weighed heavily as I grieved with family after Iraena's disappearance. Auckland, the place where my sisters and I grew up, was so full of memories, and everywhere I turned brought another recollection that strangled my broken heart. I was shattered on every level.

Auckland city life became hopeless to me at that time, reminding me of my sister, reminding me of the people who had failed her, how I had failed her. Three weeks after my sister disappeared from my life, I realised that I needed to get away, far away from Auckland, far away from this haunted home.

The best place to do that was in my tribal lands. I wanted to be in nature with healing water surrounding me. I wanted to bathe alone by the river and cry streams to eternity. I wanted to be close to my ancestors and their protection. I wanted a safe refuge to rest

20 Māori Word for tribe.

in my ancestor´s *Korowai*[21] that would engulf me in love and light. My heart was broken, and I wanted to go home to my true home *mana whenua*[22].

I went with my cousin to an off-the-grid space where we stayed in a simple dwelling built by local families in the rainforest of Te Ure wera. *Whare Manaaki*[23] was a sanctuary with no electricity; water came from a freshwater spring from a mountain above. There are a few ways to get there. One is by foot, the other by horse. The third option is a small boat up the river, but that option only exists when the river tide is at the right height.

My cousin and I walked, and my feet ached because I had decided to walk barefoot up the riverbed for many hours, wanting to absorb the healing waters all I could. As I tried to sleep that night, I tossed and turned, my monkey mind jumping from one thought to the next. I heard the rich rainforest sounds outside, the flowing river, waterfalls in the distance and the night insects resounding. As if by some miracle, for the first time since I had landed back in New Zealand, I drifted off into a deep sound sleep, lulled in the healing arms and sounds of Mother Nature.

I flew over rivers, oceans, and mountains. I flew like the rush of a golden eagle on the currents of wind. The sun was shining the brightest summer light, I had to shield my eyes. I was exhilarated, free. Then in a split second I was sitting at a beach, with my sister Iraena Rama Te Awhina. It was a sunny day, and she was holding my hand and smiling at me. I was so relieved.

Here you are.

Then suddenly, a rush of thoughts and questions raced through me.

"What happened? You were gone. Tell me everything. Please."

She was shining so bright, gorgeous and peaceful, illuminated in white light and wearing a flowing white dress.

---

21 Māori cloak.

22 Māori term for the pride lands, tribal lands.

23 Healing home in Māori

She just smiled at me and said, *"It's OK."*

I was blinded when I looked at her, she was so effulgent. It seemed as if her entire beautiful form was the pure embodiment of sunlight. There was a deep sense of calm and peace around her. All my panic and questions melted away. We sat together and she stroked my face with an angelic softness.

"I really love you; you are so lovely." She smiled.

"I love you too." I replied.

We embraced, absorbed in this bright healing sunlight. Then in a flash like a thunderbolt I landed back into my body with full force. My heart sank as I jolted back into consciousness. I didn't want this to end. A thousand thoughts raced through my head as tears flooded my eyes in torrents. I knew that it was goodbye, that I would never be with her in her physical body ever again. I cried for my loss, I cried for everything. I cried in pain, I cried whole, rushing rivers of tears. I was inconsolable.

At sunrise I got up and walked out of the healing home. The sun was just coming up from behind the mountains, warming the lands. I walked a ways and sat down on the banks of the river. The thick mist was still covering the lands like a beautiful, soft, kind blanket. There was a deep spiritual presence hovering with me; I was closer to God than ever before. I made a promise that morning.

I spoke to God. Until that point, I was very angry, upset that he could have allowed this to happen. Why didn't he protect her? Why did he do this to us? In this moment by the river, comforted by the mist, a sense of momentary freedom fell over me.

Events in life are often out of our control, not up to us to affect or change. We cannot understand matters of the heart and soul with our logical minds, the how and why of occurrences. I made a promise and sat down to pray.

> *"Dear Lord, I will try my utmost every day, to surrender to your will. To accept all the good and bad that is given to me and to devote my life to helping others reconnect to their mind-body-soul purpose. I know you are with me, please make me your instrument. Let me remember your love and light through all my darkest times. I have nothing but you."*

One of the most spectacular waterfalls on the planet is in the Tuhoe tribal lands. It rumbles with an unstoppable force. In Māori tradition we bathe in holy waters in nature: ocean, rivers, lakes, hot springs, or waterfalls. Plunging into these waters we absorb the water's energy, it's great ancient wisdom. We are purified. I was able to experience a great sense of healing in these first few months after my sister had passed away, living in the Tuhoe tribal lands, bathing in ancient waters, soothing my broken heart.

This was the only safe place for me at this time of great struggle and inner turmoil, trauma, and distress. The healing power of Mother nature was my integral strength and medicine at the time I needed it the most. Bathing in these waters brought me hope and a glimmer of peace. I wished the same for my sister and felt that somehow her soul was with me through water; our souls united again in the ripples of the healing waters we both so loved.

My mission became more clearly defined once my sister passed away. I could not save her, yet I had an opportunity to dedicate my life to helping other women in the world. Through the variety of healing modalities, I had learned from the Yoga traditions and the healing traditions. I knew every day of my life moving forward, that I would be devoted to women's wellness, to helping unite mind-body-spirit. This *'fierce grace'*[24] was now upon me. Fierce because it was the most intense time in my life, yet the grace that was emerging allowed me to connect deeper to spirit than ever before.

Ta moko is an ancient tradition of the Māori and Polynesian people. It is, in practice, a tattoo, though it is much more than that: it is a rite of passage and a deep healing experience. At the time we lost our sister, my younger sister, Lainie Elizabeth Sky, and I decided it was time to honour this tradition. I had two tattoos already from my teenage years.

The *Ta moko* tradition is much more complex than a tattoo and comes from ancient wisdoms of the Māori people. At the initial meeting, the *Ta Moko* specialists delved into our ancestral history and the reason why we wanted to participate in the rite. In the traditional sense of *Ta moko,* you must have a reason for the procedure – not simply to get a cool design on your body.

24 "Fierce grace" is a documentary memoir of Ram Dass' journey and stroke, from 2001.

The *Ta Moko* specialists already knew something of our ancestry from the tribes we are from. The Māori people pride themselves on ancestral history. Each tribe also has specific and key presiding divinities. In our case this was the goddess Hinepukohurangi - The Goddess of the Mist, who came that fate-filled day when my sister left her physical body. One of her lovers, Uenuku – the God of Rainbows, is also depicted. Someone who knows the ancient Māori symbology would be able to recognise from the patterns, where we are from and what the depictions represent.

The Southern cross is a constellation of four stars in the Southern hemisphere which have great spiritual and navigational significance for the Māori people. We are four sisters representing each of those four stars. We discussed other symbolism, and then gave time for the *Ta Moko* specialists to meditate upon the unique *Ta Moko* that they would prepare for us.

Serious *Ta moko* artists devote their lives to art and ritual. After speaking with us they told us that the three of them would work together on designing our unique *Ta moko.* When we came back a few weeks later to see the design that they had prepared, we were in awe of the depth of thought and story interwoven within these sacred symbols.

The time came for Lainie and I to begin our *Ta moko* ceremony. We had decided that we would mark the left side of our bodies, the feminine side in many ancient cultures worldwide. We were honouring our sister. We began as every endeavour does in the Māori tradition, with prayers in our original language of New Zealand *Te Reo Māori.*

As we sat with our eyes closed, the artists called upon the guiding lights of our ancestors to heal and protect us all. As soon as one of them began his *karakia*[25], I saw an array of colours with my inner eye, light flooding down into all of us. The intensity was strong, like

25 Māori for prayer

I had experienced in the Taoist cave of China earlier that year. Yet this time the intensity did not bother me.

My heart was bubbling with a safe healing love. There are no words that can describe the ineffable love energy that was pouring forth, it was as if the angels had flown down from heaven to shower us with this divine light, so needed and so comforting for us weary and broken sisters.

As we lay down for the next part of the *Ta moko* imprinting process, I felt so much gratitude to be a part of this ancient ceremony, the healing energy continuing to flood in and around me. I told my *Ta moko* artist that he did not need to use an outline of the *Ta moko* design on me, but rather to go free hand. I remember the buzzing of the machine and needle, though I was in an altered state of awareness.

The *Ta moko* artist who worked with me was surprised, many hours into the process, that I had not asked for a break. The *Ta moko* process creates a physical scar, a wound. But the wound in my heart and soul that had not yet scarred over was so deep that no physical pain could affect me.

The *Ta moko* blessing was one of the greatest blessings and initiations of my life, a great honour and privilege to be a part of an ancient process that was still just as powerful as it was aeons ago. To this day, the beautiful patterns and stories in my *Ta moko* bring me to tears, evoke such love and gratitude. The scar of losing my sister had become the most beautiful story on my body.

Never before had the ancient Vedic Mantras been sung in the traditional Māori meeting houses of New Zealand. Several months after Iraena's disappearance, I happened to be in Christchurch as Krishna Das arrived on his *Kirtan*[26] singing tour, and was to perform

26 Praising the divine through song.

in a traditional *Wharenui*[27], this one called *Nga hau e wha* 'meeting house of the four winds.'

The meeting house is often referred to as a human body, with stories and spiritual significance in each carving and pillar of the structure. I sat near the front of the room, in an embrace of Māori carvings and designs. It was as if the ancestors from long ago were keeping a watchful eye on us, the people who had gathered were of all ages, Māori and *Pakeha* alike.

As Krishna Das began the first chant, it set an eerie tone. With the entire crowd he chanted "Om," the sound vibrating through my body right through to my cells. The entire structure buzzed, filled with so many voices, creating our own new sound together. I began to cry.

Every breath I took was a release of the heavy burdens I carried for not having saved my sister. A release of the dagger-like pain in my heart. This was healing Mantra-medicine. The music was amplified by a sound system so loud that I cried without embarrassment. In this inspiring, ancient Māori home I sat in healing, surrounded by ancient Indian chants resounding in every direction, around and through me.

I knew then, with full awareness, the power of Mantra, the healing power of coming together with others to sing these sacred chants, to hear our voices as one. The vibrations we created empowered us, causing tangible transformation *in that moment*. Heart-opening and mind-resting power.

I had been carrying pain in my left shoulder from the time of my sister's disappearance – it was melting away *at that moment*. The pain lodged deep in my soul, of losing my best friend, my sister, didn't disappear but I was a touch lighter. I was thankful to be feeling even a little bit of peace after so many months of suffering, in this sacred place, present to the moment.

---

27 Māori for meeting house.

There was a glimmer of 'fierce grace' that night, thanks to Krishna Das, the chanting, and the vibrating humanity that surrounded me. Nothing had essentially changed from before I walked into the *wharenui*, the world outside still held so many questions without answers. But inside, I healed just a little. I could feel my mind-body-soul connected again, and in contemplating how death brings us closer to life, I found some little piece of freedom inside of me.

This is a poem I wrote for my sister Iraena Rama Te Awhina, a small offering of words that can only express a few drops of what my heart's ocean wants to say to my sister in spirit.

Sistars 4eva

You are my soul sister, the one I always kissed ya, best wisher,
best wisher, can't help but miss her.

Thought I was untouchable
Thought I was on top of the world
Till it all came tumbling down
Tearing me from that plane & to the ground
True natural beauty, I admired you so
That's why it's so hard to let you go
In a way there is no separation
Soul sisters with inner connection
Many lifetimes with universal meaning
Even as kids we knew which story to be reading.

Tipping me on the edge of a knife
So much dreadful fear that fateful night
Time after time I was there
The one you relied on, had no fear
All those days dancing free together
Some of my greatest memories forever

In this dance, time stood still
We were flowing in trance on that hill.
There could've been a thousand people
You and I oblivious as equal.

Starlight star bright first sister I see tonight.
Holding on with all my might
Wanting to wake up from this nightmare
Feeling like the whole world didn't care
Then you came to me, in my dream
Shining bright on a sun crystal sea
You held my hand and touched my face
You told me you loved me, so much grace.
The most incredible sunlight, I could hardly see
But in that moment you set me free.

Sitting here today, the pain is still the same
I know somehow this is all the divine game.
Doesn't change the fact, I'm holding on to regret
Wishing I had saved the day, avoiding fates net.
What comforts me, is knowing you're a deep part of me
Even the Indian seer, saw two of me, WE
All the years that have passed, and how
The most magical moments still happen now.
You've opened me to my life's purpose,
God I pray that you keep me in this service.

You are my soul sister, the one I always kissed ya, best wisher, best wisher, can't help but miss her.

India pilgrimage

In 2005, a year after my sister passed, I finally made it to Vrindavan a sacred pilgrimage town in Northern India *Maha Bharat*[28]. In my very first few days in India, I awakened at crazy early hours of the morning chanting 'Radhe Radhe.' The Goddess Radha is the beloved of Krishna (God), the feminine embodiment, Krishna's Goddess. I was never an early riser, but in India I was so excited from the moment I got to Neem Karoli Baba Maharaji´s ashram.

I woke up, chanting 'Radhe Radhe Radhe Radhe.' In the lands of the Vraj area, people use the names of Radha and Krishna to say hello and goodbye. The chanting of Radha and Krishna here continues throughout the day and night. In temples, on the streets, in homes, a perceptible buzz throughout. These chants which I began singing in the US had come alive in Vrindavan. I could hear the chants inside of me – and I felt my heart more open than ever before.

At that early hour there was not a lot going on in the temple of Maharaji´s ashram, but the Hare Krishna Hare Rama singers sang all day and night, the very famous ancient mantra,

'Hare Krishna Hare Krishna, Krishna Krishna Hare Hare, Hare Rama Hare Rama, Rama Rama Hare Hare.'

Over and over twenty-four seven. No break in the chanting, only perhaps for a few seconds, while one kirtan singer replaced the

28 Maha Bharat - original name of India.

previous. Three or four men depended on a failing microphone and a bedraggled speaker that squealed intermittently, taxed as it was by power outages that happened half a dozen times a day. In secret I would revel in those times when the electricity was cut and a natural silence entered, when we sat in dark, quiet. No squealing sound system. Just the sound of the harmonium and drum along with the pure kirtan singers' voices and breath.

I imagined myself sitting in the Ram temple centuries ago, as I sang my heart out following the lead of these simple and pure-hearted temple singers who had dedicated their life to sitting and singing the same chant over and over. I tried to catch at least one of them having a nap or dozing off during the early hours, but I never did. They were always there at the temple singing and present. These men were nourished on the deepest levels of human consciousness by the mantra.

As the morning progressed, other ashram devotees emerged from the shadows in fresh garments having just bathed, ready to serve in the various temples and shrines within the ashram compound. At around 5am, it was time for the morning *Aarti,* waving of fire lamp lights in the final resting place, the *Samadhi* of the great saint Maharaji.

The loud bells sounded, from round metal discs like gongs, so loud it dominated the space with its 'DING DING DONG DONG!'

As the newest arrival, I was assigned this instrument to play every morning, but after a few mornings of its insistent DING DONG, my ears were splitting, and I indicated that I preferred to clap my hands in rhythm instead, and sing along, as it was much more natural to me. They seemed pleased with my choice and handed me small handheld jingle bells, which would be easier to handle and so much sweeter sounding.

I felt at home here in the ashram with the Indian and Western devotees. I was happy to be a part of the ashram's daily life and rituals, no longer a tourist observing. It was easy to become part of this community. The warm friendliness of the ashram was inspiring, the community I longed for in life; the ignited, compassionate, and inspiring people I had tried to move towards my whole life. India was like home to me from the day I arrived: ease in the air, joy in the sounds, divine sights, a peaceful presence allowing me to go deeper both inward and outward.

The ashram workers were gentle, happy and simple. There was never any observable drama. Everyone seemed to do their assigned duties happily. From the ashram manager to the Hanuman temple priest. Shared responsibility and kindness made things work well here. Maharaji at the centre of all their lives. I knew without a doubt this was my new home.

Māori prayer of thanks I wrote when I arrived in Vrindavan 2005.

Ko Io te timatanga nei
Ko Ranginui e tu nei
Ko Papatuanuku ki raro nei
Nga Kaitiaki o te whenua
Ko Krishna raua ko Radha
Tena koutou
Ko Yamuna Devi te awa
Ko Giri Raaj te Maunga
Nga tipuna o Vrindavan
Tena koutou
Ko Neem Karoli Baba te kaitiaki o te wahi tapu tenei
Huri noa I tou tatau whare
Tena koutou, Tena koutou, Tena koutou katoa
Ka kitea te wairua tapu
Te ngakau, te mokohiti o te ia toto
Ka whakamoeiti ka whaka
Kororia kia kaha te pikina ki te aroha

HAUMIE HUIE TAIKIE E

This is the divine beginning
The God of sky above
Mother Earth below
The guardians of the lands
Radha and Krishna
Greetings to you
The river is Yamuna Devi
The mountain is Giri Raaj
Ancestors of Vrindavan
Greetings to you all
Neem Karoli Baba is the guardian of this sanctuary
All around his home
Greetings greetings greetings to you all
The holy spirit is seen
The heart and life force energy
Are present and validate what is
Glory to being strong as you rise in love

After a few days in Vrindavan, I discovered the Yamuna ji river about half an hour walk from Maharaji´s ashram. I wanted to walk to the river, and recalled my walks in the New Zealand rainforest, accompanied by Tui birds and towering trees. In India, though, it is difficult as a non-Indian woman to walk alone. It can feel like being stalked. Curious people follow, sometimes speaking or wanting to touch. I found it impossible to get any peace or quiet contemplation and study time by the river Yamuna. So I came up with a cunning plan.

I would disguise myself as a boy, in the hope that as I walked to the sacred waters, I may be left alone. History holds so many stories of women who had to protect themselves in different ways. I was happy to play dress up as a boy if it gave me the peace I so desired.

The next morning, I put a wrap-around *lungi* (cloth men use) around my waist covering my legs, and a bound style *bundi* shirt on top, wrapped my head in a turban-like cloth to cover my hair, and another shawl around my shoulders. Every inch a young boy.

I chanted quietly to myself and kept my eyes down, watching only my bare feet raise the dust along a path that I knew so well. As I made my way through the fields that led to the river, I broke out in a smile. My disguise had worked. Not a single person had followed me. I wanted to jump up and down for joy and scream out what the locals say *'Jai ho'* – All glories – but I didn't want my *lungi* to come off or my *bundi* to fall open! I kept my New Zealand practice of diving into the sacred waters in check, sitting quietly to study.

I was just beginning to learn the *Shri Yamunashtakam* and began to chant. This eight-verse Sanskrit prayer was written by *Shri Vallabhacharya Mahaprabhuji*[29] in praise of Shri Yamuna ji the goddess, and the river named after her. The first time I heard this chant, it gave me a warm feeling inside. From that moment I was determined to learn this prayer. With honour and respect sitting on the banks of the Shri Yamuna ji river I began to sing.

Namami Yamuna maham
Sakala siddhi hetu muda…

I bow praise and honour you Yamuna ji the giver of all divine powers…

Shri Yamunaji is said to appear for her devoted ones to remove their obstacles. The Goddess of Grace, she allows her devotees to conquer their lower nature, and allows divine souls to enter into the path of grace. Sitting on the banks of the river, her waters sparkling, peaceful and perfect, I felt a great oneness with the scene unfolding before my eyes.

29 A great 16th century teacher and visionary leader, the founder of the Pushtimarg tradition otherwise known as 'The path of Grace.' Also see endnotes.

Silky swallows swooped, dancing and cooing to rhythms only they could hear. The scene was in perfect harmony, a momentary paradise on Earth. I didn't care what day of the week it was or what month. At the bank of the river, I was full with the excitement of having found a home in India. I looked forward to making my way down to the soft sandy banks of Yamuna every morning, to recite her prayer over and over, uninterrupted until I knew it all by heart.

Namami Yamuna maham
Sakala siddhi hetu muda…

Shyamdas was a revolutionary devotional writer, Sanskrit scholar, translator, singer and beloved Bhakta[30] of the Pushtimarg[31] tradition. I met Shyamdas in my early twenties at the Omega Ecstatic chant weekend in Rhinebeck, New York. We were introduced by my friend Krishna Das.

Shyamdas was born in the US to a Russian Jewish family. He left for India when he was 19 years old in search of a spiritual path. He had met some of the Ram Dass people and headed off in the hope of meeting great teachers in India. When we met he had been living in India for almost 40 years.

Shyamdas´ first words to me were in *Gujarati*[32], assuming I was Indian. I was dumbfounded. What was he saying? When he realised that I did not understand him, he spoke to me in English. Krishna Das arranged my accommodation for the weekend, at Shyamdas´ home in Woodstock.

I occupied a small house in his garden, where I woke to birds singing and the smiling sun. After a cup of warm chai tea, a friend and I made our way down to the Hudson River which ran alongside Shyamdas´ property.

We wrangled through an overgrown path in the woods and meandered down to the riverbank. I prayed and sang songs in Māori honouring the nature spirits and the river, a tradition I learned in New Zealand growing up. My friend told me that the Bhakti tradition of Pushtimarg also has Sanskrit prayers and songs sung to honour holy rivers and places. Naturally I was intrigued. Then, of course, a full dive into the river waters. I felt cleansed, revitalised and refreshed.

As we sang the Sanskrit line in praise of the river, Shyamdas arrived on the scene, dressed in a *dhoti*[33]. He prayed quickly and touched the water of the river to his eyes and head before diving

30 Devotee of the divine

31 Path of grace lineage established by Shri Vallabhacharya 16th century.

32 A northern Indian dialect.

33 Traditional flowing cloth for men.

in. I could not help wondering how he could swim in all the cloth that was floating around him from his dhoti.

"Chalo" Shyamdas said as he gracefully glided out of the water. "Let's go!" And, ah, the dhoti cloth was still attached.

It was time for breakfast and my tummy was ready and rumbling. Shyamdas laid out plates on his back porch and served his famous *Thakor-ji prasad.* Prasad is holy sanctified food that is offered to God. Prasad can be understood as the grace or nourishment of God, in the form of the food we were about to enjoy.

What a feast! Fluffy pancakes dribbling with delectable maple syrup, fresh berries and bananas. Bright avocado and quinoa salad shining in rainbow colours. Silky blueberry smoothie. I was in heaven.

Shyamdas looked at me and asked "So, what do you think of the prasad?"

"Can I be honest?" I smiled.

"Sure, we like honesty in this house." He jeered me on.

"Well, I have to say that first, I have never met a man who can cook this well, and second, this prasad as you call it, is so divine that I really want more. These are the best pancakes I have ever had in my life." I was in bliss.

"Good," he said, smiling with a twinkle in his eye. "You can stay." He served more exquisite prasad. I was content in my mind, body, heart and tummy. There was deep acceptance and trust in the air that morning.

This was the beginning of my relationship with Shyamdas. In one day he had become my best friend. He was always gracious and generous to all who crossed his path. Whether serving people prasad or teaching grace-filled lessons on Bhakti, he had the ability to see the greatest spiritual potential in everyone, long before they could even see it in themselves. He had the gift of wishing well for all he met. I was introduced to Bhakti practises in a deep way by hanging out with Shyamdas.

Over many years we spent a portion of every year together, mostly in the sacred lands of Vraj, the Vrindavan area which Shyamdas liked to call *Radha Krishna land.* Their dance of love exists in all of creation. In Radha Krishna land the love of God was everywhere.

The love poetry of the Pushtimarg was intriguing to me. As soon as I heard Shyamdas singing the unique *Dhrupad Haveli*[34] sangeet style Kirtan, I was fascinated, it sent shivers up my spine. This was the first Pushtimarg Kirtan I learned and was written by the well-known great 16th Century poet, *Suradas*[35].

This particular poem was in the language of *Vrajwasha*[36]. When sung with such love and depth by my God brother Shyamdas, I was eager to learn, it was hypnotising. We walked together through the holy Radha Krishna lands often reciting this love poem, over and over until it was deep inside my heart consciousness.

Shri Yamuna ji tiharo darsha mohi bhave
Shri Gokula ke nikata bahata ho
laharana ki chabi ave

sukha karani dukha harani
Shri Yamuna ji, jo jana prata uta nave
Madana Mohan ju ki, kariye Pyarey
Pata Rani ju kahave

Shri Vrindavana mae Raasa rachorye
Mohana murali Bhajave..
Suradas Prabhu tihari milana ko
veda vimala yasha gave

34 Dhrupad Haveli Sangeet - Classical Indian music form.

35 Suradas, see endnotes.

36 Vrajwasha - sanskrit based Vraj Northern India dialect.

Sri Yamuna ji I desire your divine vision on your banks in Shri Gokul, and I want to see the beautiful ripples of your water.

You give pleasure to all and remove suffering
Shri Yamuna ji, I immerse myself in your waters
You are the beloved wife of the supreme beloved enchanter of hearts.

In Shri Vrindavan where the divine love nectar dance takes place by the call of the beloved´s flute.

Suradas wish´s to meet with this one, who's glory is sung of in the Vedas.

It is in this Radha Krishna space with Shyamdas, where I experienced a profound shift in my consciousness, and met some of the most captivating, inspirational, and enlightening people of my life. Barefoot we wandered the sacred pilgrimage sites of Vraj and visited holy places. My life transformed.

I was enchanted by the ways of the great teachers and simple household practitioners alike. Rich or poor, old or young, these teachers lived in a state of blissful absorption in God. Even just to sit with these Bhakti practitioners was heart opening as the mind chatter ceased effortlessly.

"Like a wet cloth will soak a dry one that is put next to it, in the same way when you are put next to a great soul you too become drenched."

- Shri Harirayji

Vishnu Shastri ji

Early on in Vrindavan I met one of my great teachers of the Bhakti Yoga path. Vishnu Shastri ji or Panditji as we affectionately called him. We were driving along a dusty road in the middle of what seemed to be nowhere, and Shyamdas told the driver to stop the car. I wondered what on Earth we were doing.

"It's Panditji, my Sanskrit teacher," Shyamdas said with excitement as he bumbled out of the car to greet him.

Their animated conversation sounded rhythmic and poetic, like a song of words pulsating, though I understood none of it. Shyamdas introduced me with the name he had given me: Mayuri Devi, "Peacock Devi."

Panditji looked me straight in the eyes and blasted me. The Sanskrit and Vrajwasha he spoke seemed to explode with conviction. I was flustered – why was he shouting at me? Perhaps I had done something out of custom? Maybe I was supposed to cover my head in front of him? Embarrassed, I looked at Shyamdas and he smiled.

Shyamdas laughed, "He's not angry. It's just the way he talks!"

Shyamdas told Panditji that I thought he was angry. Now Panditji was laughing. Relieved, I laughed, too.

"He wants to tell you a few things. I will translate for you." Shyamdas smiled.

Panditji continued in his booming display of Sanskrit and Vrajwasha as he stared into my eyes. His eyes were covered with black kajal, a natural ayurvedic black eyeliner powder that seemed to make the glance in his deep brown eyes sparkle even brighter. I dared not look away. His forehead was covered in yellow sandalwood paste and smeared with red kum kum powder on his third eye. I was spellbound by his aura and presence. His commanding wisdom permeated the air, he had me entranced, unlike any other human being I would ever encounter. His voice sounded like rhythmic thunder, powerful and poetic.

He continued booming his words. Shyamdas translated with great reverence in his voice.

"You are Vrajdevi, you are meant to be here, this is your home. You will always be here, you will never leave." All the while giving Shyamdas hand gestures to translate to me.

The original Vrajdevis were women of Vraj who lived at the time of Shri Krishna. The epic *Bhagavata Purana*[37] speaks of them. They are said to be the greatest Bhaktas who hold the highest banner of

37 Ancient Sanskrit text that gives details of Krishna and his associates.

love and devotion to Krishna. They are revered in Bhakti traditions as the Guru of Gurus on the Bhakti path. I had no idea at the time what an honour it was to carry their name and aspire to such devotion. This instant empowerment Panditji had blessed me with the name of these great empowered Bhaktas, bestowing upon me his greatest hopes and blessings. In giving me this name, he gifted me the best example to follow.

"You are Vrajdevi and you will learn to live like them, your life will change. You need to start by learning Sanskrit and Vrajwasha." I could tell from the force of his words, and Shyamdas' expression, that this was not a dialogue. He was instructing me, commanding me even.

After only about three days in India, I suddenly had this path. Sanskrit? One of the hardest languages in the world? The script alone is baffling. Not for this girl who spoke only English and a little bit of Māori. Impossible.

But great souls like Panditji see straight to one's soul purpose. He saw my greatest potential before I could even imagine it, before I could even understand it. That day he blessed me with a vision for my life purpose, is a day forever etched in my heart. I had met a true teacher. My first Sanskrit Guru.

When I left New Zealand after losing my sister, I wanted to be a part of a community, part of my own spiritual revolution. Within a few months I met Shyamdas in the US, and through him made discoveries in India. Now meeting his beloved Panditji on this day made my heart sing. I trusted Shyamdas, and through him his teacher. I was becoming part of something very special; I just had no idea what it was. But I was excited to find out.

Sometime later I discovered that Panditji was a renowned Sanskrit scholar and used to be the head Principal at a school of Sanskrit. He was from a specific Brahman Priest class called *Chobe Brahmans* of the Vraj mandal area. He was the Guru to the Gurus, a Sanskrit encyclopaedia of the ancient wisdoms of the Bhakti paths.

He had memorised mammoth volumes of sacred texts and devoted his life to *satsang*[38]. He was generous with sharing his wisdom to all, from great Gurus to the flower lady behind the temple. His wisdom, infused with divine awareness and experience, gave him the aspect of a person fully embodying the path of grace-filled devotion.

Listening to Panditji inspired deep respect. Watching him was entrancing. Feeling the esoteric teachings that emanated from him, I knew without a doubt that I was in the presence of a Sanskrit phenomenon. He exuded not only wisdom, but also the highest Bhakti love and devotion, moving many in his *satsang* audiences to tears of bliss.

I was amazed at the speed with which I picked up the Sanskrit *stotra*[39] and mantra chanting, along with the heart-warming Vrajwasha love poems. The music and the words were somehow familiar to me, and I was hypnotised by these sacred jewels. I became dedicated to Panditji's words. I met with him every few days, and he kept informed of my progress. I aimed to do my very best as my path of Bhakti Yoga began. I was inspired to learn and absorb all the drops of nectar I discovered on this path.

I became infused with Sanskrit vibrations. Baffling as it was to me – my consciousness absorbed these ancient keys of wisdom, unlocking a vast, infinite ocean filled with waves of love. I copied Sanskrit text in its original script along with the audio passages. It is said that when you are with enlightened company, you are affected in the most powerful and profound ways.

These ancient secrets came to me in unconventional ways: I attended no classroom or institution. They came to me in the fields of potential. In the seeds of sincerity. From the minds of masters. In the hearts of healers. In the determination of dedication. In the breath of sound. Sanskrit was being downloaded into me at the core of my being.

38 Enlightened conversation and gatherings of people in uplifting settings.

39 A hymn of praise melodically sung.

A memory of Panditji that I keep close aptly portrays his vast ability to inspire.

It was India's afternoon nap time, but I didn't feel like napping. I was energised and headed to my favourite spot on the rooftop for quiet contemplation and meditation. As I made my way outside towards the 500-year-old staircase that leads to the roof. I was surprised to see Panditji sitting up, not in his usual snoring nap posture. He called me over. Frustrated that I wouldn't have my quiet time, and fearful that he would task me with laundry or some other chore I didn't want to do, I hoped to distract him.

"Panditji, can I get you some water? Some sweets?"

He motioned me to sit down in front of him.

"You just sit here and listen to what I am going to tell you." He commanded in his usual way.

His eyes sparkled with truth and wisdom. I was always fully transfixed when he spoke. Time suspended, he was speaking much slower than usual, and I could easily understand everything he said in Vrajwasha. He told me many things, he spoke of esoteric teachings. He spoke of the importance of what I needed to learn. He wanted me to commit wholeheartedly to everything he was advising me.

This was the first ever one-to-one *satsang* I had ever had with him. I felt privileged to have solo time with him, surrounded as he was so often by devotees. A rush of love flooded over me, in the presence of one who had full awareness of the ultimate divine reality. There was so much love and respect bubbling forth, it felt as if my heart was going to burst out of my chest and explode. Though there were to be many more moments of personal connection with my dear teacher, I hold this first *satsang* alone as a true blessing.

Panditji held me accountable as no one had before, drumming his wisdom into me by gentle force. He smacked the top of my head, blessing me and spoke to me in English for the first time.

"You are my daughter; I am your old father. Old, yeah, old."

He laughed a great big belly laugh. I laughed too, through tears of joy and reverence in that moment. Serious and sweet timeless moments of Panditji wisdom, on waves of love.

Biharvan is a temple and ashram, about an hour's drive from Vrindavan. Hundreds of pure white cows live in a huge *Goshala*[40]. These cows are said to be descendants of Nanda Baba's cows. Nanda Baba was the father of Krishna, and herded cows in Vrindavan many thousands of years ago. Only a few monks live in Biharvan now, tending to their beloved cows.

My God brother, Vallabhdas, and I arrived one afternoon during a quiet period, a kind of spiritual siesta. No one was around, and the main temple was closed, so we took this opportunity to wander into their private walled forest/garden. There was an unusual, alluring quiet hanging in the air. We were pleased to have arrived at just the right time for undisturbed exploration.

Wandering through, we encountered no one. We scaled the boundary wall of the temple grounds and found space along the brick wall of the garden to relax in the shade of Pipal and Kadamba trees. I closed my eyes and mused about our good fortune to have found this contemplative space. As happened so often during my time in India, every day was a new adventure, seemingly guided by divine orchestration.

The sun was starting to lower, and we heard bells in the distance, signalling the start of afternoon worship in the temple. I popped up like a rabbit, eager to make our way toward the bells. The temple doors opened, and a mix of monks, *sadhus*[41], and village people gathered around calling out.

"Jai Ho, Jai ho."

40 Cow sanctuary

41 A holy person, who has renounced worldly life, dedicated to a spiritual path.

Praising the forms of Krishna inside the Goshalla temple.

They waved small ghee lamps of fire in front of the main deities, singing. This *Aarti* rite is beautiful: young and old, singing, ringing bells, playing instruments. They have come for the *darshan*[42]. Though I couldn't decipher the words, the melody was mesmerising and the *bhav*[43] was pure bliss. Even the many who sang off-key did it with such love and devotion. As this *Aarti* ended, everyone bowed to the ground in great reverence and respect for this temple, and then quickly dispersed.

Afterwards, one of the *sadhus* invited us to meet the resident teacher - *Guru Maharaj*[44]. We accepted with flooding enthusiasm. We had been waiting all day for the next part of this adventure to unfold, as it always does in magical India.

We followed the *sadhu* named Ramdas through a courtyard and to a rooftop apartment where a few chosen people had gathered. A withered man sat on an Indian-style bed, low to the ground. We prostrated and paid our respects to the Guru Maharaj, then sat in the back. It was getting dark, and there was no electricity in this ancient temple. One of the devotees lit a candle and placed a few around the Guru's daybed. We could not see his face in the dark. He spoke in a deep masculine voice yet sweet and sincere to the ears.

Everything felt tinged with mystery. The candlelight, his speech that I could not understand... Yet the *bhav* mood in the room was of pure love and contentment. His words sounded poetic – rhythmic and hypnotic. Vallabhdas translated a few words he recognized – the Guru spoke to us of chanting the names of God and becoming absorbed in this love.

Vallabhdas was picking up the languages much faster than I. He had a genius-like quality about him. We sat in this glowing candlelight terrace, contemplating the love of God, a few peacocks

42 Divine sight through worship.

43 Devotional feeling/mood.

44 Guru Maharaj, name used throughout India for various teachers, is an affectionate name for a Guru, used by their followers.

calling in the distance their final goodnight before all was hidden under the shawl of night.

After some time, Ramdas who had invited us, signalled for us to depart. We followed him outside, to where a few other *sadhus* had started a small fire behind the main temple. We were invited to sit with them, on the soft silky sands called Vraj Raj which are famous all over the Vrindavan Vraj area. The *sadhus* began to sing late night *Kirtan* praise filled love songs.

With a drum and a few shakers and bells these *sadhus* sang with such love and devotion. We were transported thousands of years back, into an ancient realm of such mystery that I wanted to stay for eternity. Vallabhdas reminded me that our ashram temple was still an hour drive away and the main gates may be locked before we get in. We recalled the difficulty we'd had waking anyone to let us in when this has happened a number of times. It was time to depart, so with great reluctance we paid our respects to the gathering of *sadhus* and went off to find the taxi in the dark.

The taxi driver had been waiting all afternoon for us, and was eager to leave. He appeared to be somewhat annoyed – none of us had planned to stay that long. He yelled at us in a bold voice typical of that region. Not knowing the language at this moment was a blessing. We smiled and he seemed relieved after his short rant.

As we were about to depart, an old *sadhu* knocked on the window of our taxi. We opened the window, as it appeared he wanted to ride with us. He jumped into the front seat of the taxi, and kept up a one-sided, animated conversation with us for a few minutes as the taxi rolled forward. His brown eyes sparkled as we smiled and smiled back, all we could offer, as we didn't understand a word he said in his thick Vrajwasha dialect.

We had not eaten since lunch, and my stomach grumbled. I hoped no one heard, as I dreamt of the delicious, thick Vraj-style *rotis* - flat breads of the region. I could just about taste one, feel its soft pillow on my tongue. My imagination would have to suffice until we got back to our ashram. After about five minutes in the taxi, the *sadhu* turned to us and asked the driver to stop. He looked at us intently, tears of love in his eyes, reaching into his bag to present us with exactly that delicious treat, a puffy roti slathered in butter and sweet on the inside.

He offered the bread to us. I tried to give it back to him, not wanting to deprive him of his dinner, but he refused and held his hands in a blessing gesture. He then sang the names of God to us the Vrindavan way to say *hello* and *goodbye* and popped open the car door and stood with folded hands at his heart as we drove off.

'Radhe Radhe Radhe Radhe'

I wanted to hold that roti in the palm of my hands just a little longer. The *sadhu* was an unexpected teacher of selflessness. We had not known him before and would probably never see him again. He gave up the only thing he had in that moment, with selfless love, offered to strangers.

> *"Discover that nothing is too small for clear vision, too insignificant for tender strength.*
>
> *Use outlook and insight, use them both and you are immune. For you have witnessed eternity."*
>
> – *unknown*

Shyamdas arranged for us to take a train to Mumbai to visit the grandson of his Guru, Goswami Milan Baba. When we arrived at the Guru's *Haveli*[45], people swarmed everywhere. Shyamdas had told us that they were celebrating the Guru's daughter's first birthday,

45 Traditional Indian temple home.

and the space overflowed with devotees, creating a joyous noise, as is customary in India. We followed Shyamdas up some stairs into a lounge, where the Guru and his family were seated.

Shyamdas and others bowed, paying respects and touching the Guru family's feet. I stood on the side not knowing what to do. I watched and smiled. This didn't last long, and before long we were back downstairs amidst the very loud singing and dancing in honour of the Guru's daughter, Raja. When the party ended, I was able to take some time with the Guru's very beautiful wife. Back in their quarters again, she looked just like a queen in her beautiful saree and jewelled adornments. To my surprise, I found that she spoke some English. We had been in rural India all this time, learning and listening to Sanskrit, Hindi, and Vrajwasha. It was sweet and appreciated that she spoke to me in English.

After the party, we enjoyed the most sumptuous *Maha Prasad*[46]. Many delectable offerings had been prepared and we were enjoying the leftovers of Krishna. After feasting on three lentil soup dhals, five sweet and savoury rice dishes, innumerable *mithai* sweets from halva to sweet balls, it was time to leave. We rolled our way into the taxi so full from the feast, and contented we made our way back to our accommodation.

On the ride back, Shyamdas and the other devotees talked with glee about the elaborate celebrations. To be honest, at that point I was quite overwhelmed by the noise, the press of so many people. Shyamdas asked me if I wanted to be initiated. He was one of the first westerners to be initiated into this path back in the 1970's.

He said I could be initiated into the path of Pushtimarg by Baba, receive a sacred mantra, and thus commit to that path. Shyamdas told me that it could happen the next day if I wanted. We had discussed initiation before coming to meet with Baba, though I lacked the courage to tell him how indecisive I felt. I nodded "OK," and went to my room.

46 Supreme vegetarian food offered in the temple and then taken as nourishment of God.

That night I tossed and turned thinking about the day, about Gurus and what it all meant. I thought about Maharaji, as he was the only Indian Guru I had known about. I thought about the Maharaji devotees I knew, and the things they told me about their experiences with their Guru. I had read a book by Ram Dass about the experiences he and his friends had had with Maharaji.

Some of it was real and beautiful, but some of it seemed beyond my understanding and belief. Since I could not sleep, I got up and turned on the light. I thought if this Baba was going to be my Guru, then I would need to ask him some questions before I would take initiation. I had only just met him that day. I needed to get to know him and see if he really was meant to be my Guru. I sat frantically writing a few questions till the early hours of the morning.

"What is a true Guru?"

"What is the relationship between Guru and disciple?"

"How do I know you are my Guru?"

The next morning, I folded my questions into a tight package, and slipped it carefully inside my little handbag. When we arrived at the Guru's *Haveli*, it was very quiet with only a couple of devotees sitting around, a complete contrast to the day before. When we reached the top of the *Haveli* on the fourth floor, Baba was waiting for us.

We sat down in front of him, and Shyamdas started a conversation in Hindi. I rummaged through my little bag trying to find the folded paper with my questions. Where was it? I know I had put it in here, only a few hours ago.

Shyamdas then turned to me and said.

"Baba wants to talk to you."

Everything was happening so fast. I kept fumbling around for the paper with my questions. Shyamdas motioned me to come and sit in front. I sat down in front of Baba.

He surprised me when he said "Shyamdas said you have some questions for me?" I had not told Shyamdas about my list.

When I looked into his eyes, I could feel my heart pounding, a lump in my throat. I was flustered from losing my questions that I had so carefully contemplated the night before. His glance upon me became intense, I knew I had to say something. I am not usually lost for words, and I managed to scramble something together.

"Yes, Baba I want to ask you some questions, but for some reason I have misplaced the paper where I had written those questions."

Baba then responded, "It's OK, you can ask me anything you wish."

I looked at Shyamdas, I looked at Baba. Both of them were smiling at me, and I felt their encouragement. Shyamdas thought so highly of Baba, and I thought the world of Shyamdas. There was no room left for me to doubt, and in that moment, I requested to be initiated, just like that.

Baba spoke a mantra into my left ear. The earth didn't shake, there were no golden lights, nothing had essentially changed, but in that moment, I knew that everything *had* changed. That initiation was the beginning of a great transformation in my life. At that time very few westerners had been initiated into this Pushtimarg *Path of Grace* lineage, a secret and sacred Bhakti sect of India.

I was ready to follow in the footsteps of someone like Shyamdas, a great Bhakta who was a huge inspiration to me. I was already on the path of Bhakti and had been living in Vrindavan for two months already. Now this initiation was confirmation to me that my path of Bhakti was sanctified.

In the popular ISKON[47] Hare Krishna movement most of the devotees are Westerners, in the Pushtimarg they are predominantly Indians. It is a more secret and hidden path – and for me, it seemed like an intriguing secret sacred path. My heart yearned with intrigue to delve deeper into my chosen path of grace. Later I would hear devotees say, when referring to entrance into this tradition:

> *"You are chosen by God. You have always been his, now you have come home to him again."*

Shyamdas was the very first non-Indian devotee to be welcomed and initiated into this path back in the early 70´s. In the first few days after arriving in Vrindavan India, Shyamdas, through divine orchestration, encountered a devotee from the Path of Grace tradition. This devotee was Mangaldas, and he offered Shyamdas a place

47 ISKON, International society for krishna consciousness. Founder Bhakti Vedanta Swami Srila Prabhupad.

to stay in their small ashram, only a few minutes' walk away, along the Vrindavan path to Neem Karoli Baba's ashram.

Shyamdas was 19 years old. Staying with this devotee, he became absorbed in *satsang,* developing a keen sense of awareness and delving deeper into Vraj Bhakti Yoga. Only a few years later he would meet the renowned Dharma advocate, master, musician, poet and spiritual leader who would become his Guru, Goswami Prathameshji, from the first house of the Path of grace.

Shyamdas remained many years in the Vraj area, living and studying with his Guru. He wrote many recollections of his beloved teacher. One of my favourites, *Ocean of Grace,* is a collection of personal recorded discussions between Goswami Prathameshji and Shyamdas, a beautiful insight into their discussions and an incredible window into the precious relationship that exists between a true Guru and disciple.

Shyamdas became a Sanskrit scholar, and was also proficient in Hindi, Gujarati and Vrajvasha. He translated many literary works of the Path of Grace into English, some of which had never been translated before at such great length. His books are filled with astounding love poetry, accounts of grace-filled practitioners and saints, as well as ancient scriptures and commentaries. For English- reading practitioners, Indian and non-Indian alike, his books contain some of the best translations to be found to this day.

Our friendship was marked by deep spiritual wisdom-filled conversations. We nourished each other on so many levels. Shyamdas was famous for distributing his divine *Maha Prasad* to anyone who may happen to be around. Indeed, some of the best *Maha Prasad* I have ever had in my life. Nobody has ever been able to reproduce his famous Shyamdas style *dhokra*[48].

There are so many things I want to say about my friendship with Shyamdas. Even all these years after his passing, it still brings a lump to my throat and tingles in my heart to even remember his smiling

48 a lentil and rice steamed savoury cake.

eyes and face. I find it hard to express the right words, to give justice and eloquence of the nature of our bond, to all that he taught me in the most unconventional way. The warmth, the compassion, the fun and adventure, the free-flowing spontaneous spirit, the unexpected revelations, the deep scholarly insights, ecstatic impromptu singing, radical and wise, a true friend in every way.

My God brother, my God Father, my beloved friend, my benefactor, my inspiration, my unconventional teacher, the best India companion anyone could ever ask for. Shyamdas hosted an array of people in India over the years from all spectra of life including Sting, Madonna, Sharon Gannon and many more extraordinary personalities. He was a host to famous people and infamous, from the chickpea man to the flower garland maker. Everyone was welcomed into his blissful orbit.

He had the energy of a 20-year-old and the wisdom of a 150-year-old. He was always ready to serve. Whether it was serving a *Prasad* meal, or explaining an incredible Sanskrit translation, he was always involved in *satsang*, *seva*[49] and *smaran*[50].

I observed him with full attention, as he taught in unconventional ways. Over the years I saw so many people coming and going, and he always responded with his steady and all-encompassing mood.

He explained to me,

> *"Satsang, good association is the key, you want to be around people who are in a good mood."*
>
> *"Listen to everyone but download the right things."*
>
> *"You can learn something from everyone, have the inner wisdom to know what parts to hear."*

---

49 selfless service.

50 remembrance of elevated things.

All these years later, I am fortunate that his words and presence still resound within me. Time spent with Shyamdas occurred within an atmosphere of adventure, excitement, and intrigue. I never knew what lay behind the next corner, and I liked it that way.

A true Bhakta devotee and well-wisher, Shyamdas was and always will be a great inspiration to me, and to so many other people on the planet as well. When I am translating and I am stuck on a Sanskrit or Vrajwasha word, although Shyamdas is no longer physically present I feel him inside of me. He still guides and gifts me with his incredible insight, and the word and its meaning come.

The first train trip I took with Shyamdas was from a place called Mathura, on my first ever trip to India. Accompanied by a satsang *mandali*[51] of Shyamdas' friends we were to travel across India. We held first-class tickets, and I was relieved to be in a private cabin, a bit away from the noise and clutter of the rest of the train. People were packed in tight, and the din of so many languages was overwhelming. Not to Shyamdas, of course – he moved with the ease of a local, having spent so many years in India.

In the quiet of our cabin, when other devotees had left us alone to buy food from the vendors along the platform, Shyamdas turned to me.

"So Vrajdevi, tell me, what happened with your sister?"

He knew about my sister, the event, anyway – we talked about it when we met in the US just after her death. At that time I was still very raw, the trauma so close to the surface. Any time I tried to talk about it, I would end up crying, so I preferred to stay silent. I was too vulnerable. Until this moment. Shyamdas embodied such genuine caring and compassion, that it felt natural to open up to him.

51 Mandali - group

I told him from beginning to end the entire story, including all the toughest parts. I didn't leave anything out. The strength of our bond, the mist, the whale. I had never done this with anyone. I told him of my anger with the police and all who failed her. I told him about the hole she left in my entire universe. My terrible, jagged, consuming pain. It all spilled out with tears.

Shyamdas cried, too, truly feeling my pain and suffering. He didn't need to say anything. His bright blue eyes gazed deeply into mine. I was bathed in the healing compassion emanating from him. There was safety in his presence, and a sense of just a little bit of release from the trauma. Shyamdas was holding space for me and it was the first time since losing my sister that someone had done this for me. After some time, he extended his hands to hold mine and said,

> *"You love so deeply, that is why you hurt so deeply."*

On another trip, we travelled by train across the Rajasthan desert, again in a private cabin. Shyamdas, a couple of dear friends, Deva Premal and Miten, and I. The sun set, flowing like a bedazzling orange saree across the arid lands. As night darkened the sky and brought forth an ocean of stars, Deva and I climbed to our bunks. Below were the two Grand Babas (my affectionate name for the elder men). The sounds of Shyamdas and Miten giggling radiated through our little cabin, random words, singing, now and then a few lines of Beatles songs.

Their laughing became so infectious that I jumped down from my bunk to join them. They were listening on a shared headset but removed it so we could hear on a speaker. They were listening to the Beatles.

> *"Yesterday...all my troubles seemed so far away, now I need a place to hide away."*

We all chimed in, everyone singing with such depth and heart. I hadn't before had such a reaction to Beatles songs! Then Shyamdas began a divine love commentary on the lyrics; how they fit so well in the divine context. He brought the deeply spiritual to light through each word of the song. The lyrics became a mantra.

"Radhe Shyam, Radhe Radhe Radhe Radhe Shyam."

We all joined in singing from the depths of our hearts to the melody of *Yesterday*.

Over the years, I have loved different genres of music: from Madonna to Tupac, Lauren Hill to Bob Marley. When, in my early 20s, I discovered Indian mantra/kirtan music, and by the time I was sitting in this song-filled cabin on the train racing across the desert, I began to feel that commercial music like pop & hip hop was worldly and ego-based, taking me away from my true divine essence as I practised sacred Sanskrit mantra chants. I stopped listening to the commercial music of my younger days.

Filled with the divine messages that Shyamdas illuminated in the Beatles lyrics, I realised that I had been wrong to cut off my original musical loves. I observed the heartfelt *bhav* that Shyamdas, Deva and Miten were experiencing through Beatles lyrics, rhythms, melodies. I saw that all music has the potential to move the heart and soul. There is always some emotion behind it. How we view and experience it is up to the individual.

I put back my rose-coloured glasses. I put on my framework of the divine and found I too could transform even the most mundane, choosing to perceive things with love rather than disdain. The choice was mine all along. I'm thankful to have had the reminder in our warm cabin that night.

> *"However, you view and see things, will either take you closer to your goal, or take you away from it. In the realm of love, everything is possible. All is love filled, you can choose how to view it."*
>
> *–anonymous*

My teachers in that moment had appeared to me again, this time in the form of these three enlightened beloved souls. When I least expect it, lessons awaited me, just a breath away.

The little boy at the Shiva temple

Sometimes my teacher was tiny.

On a retreat that Shyamdas and I led with a Yoga teacher from the US, we stopped at a Shiva temple in the Rajasthan desert. Ready for a short break after several hours in the van, we piled out of the car – a dozen Americans, Shyamdas and I, and our two male Indian assistants.

A young boy about five years old rushed to our group. Local kids often hassle and hustle donations from groups like this. Sometimes a small army of kids follow along, looking for a way to get some coins. One becomes many and many become the army.

But this little guy was solo. I saw the American women from our group smiling and talking with him. He didn't seem to be asking for anything, but rather smiling back and keeping a respectful distance. Our tour walked along, and we spied a nearby lake for our rest stop. The little boy still followed, no other kids in sight.

We sat as a group, dotted along the edge of the lake. The little boy sat down too, near Shyamdas and me. It seemed unusual behaviour for a small seemingly homeless boy to be hanging around without harassing us. He seemed happy watching us. Shyamdas and I conversed with the boy in Hindi.

"Where are your parents?" I asked.

His legs and bare feet were covered in dust. He wore tiny brown shorts and a red and white collared shirt. His face was covered in dust too, and he had some cuts on his soft brown face. Snot was drying on his nose and cheeks. Underneath the assumed poverty, his large brown eyes sparkled. His smile was full of such sweetness, among all his wounds.

"My Papa, is him." He said pointing to the Shiva temple behind us.

Knowing for certain now that he was homeless, we asked more questions.

"Where is your home? Where do you sleep?" Shyamdas wanted to know more about this little boy.

"Over there, that is my home, you see the side of the temple there. Well, just beneath there I sleep. Can you see my blanket?" He smiled and pointed to his temple home.

He exuded such profound humility. My tears welled up, my heart engaged. This little boy, who had no parents and no home, was smiling and content with his blanket at the side of the Shiva temple. He had full faith as Shiva, an incarnation of God, watched over his every move, took care of all his needs. He seemed to feel Shiva as his own personal father.

I asked one of Shyamdas' helpers to bring *prasad* from the car for the boy. We got a leaf bowl out of the snack bag and offered him a variety of the foods we had made that morning for the trip. To my surprise, instead of scoffing down the entire lot, he paced himself. Chewing and eating slowly as he peered at us from time to time, giving us a smile. Each bite seemed amazing to him. He smiled and looked into the distance, savouring sweet simplicity.

So often there is an unsurprising desperation that accompanies the homeless children of India, displaying aggression or anger as they try to feed their needs. It happened to me once. In a small village, a desperate mob of children ambushed me for trinkets I had purchased for them in the local market. Setting upon me, pulling things from my hands, knocking me to the ground, and ripping at my saree.

That time, Shyamdas, often my saviour, yelled at the mob in Hindi and they scattered. Shyamdas pulling me up from the ground didn't scold me, only said that I will eventually learn the correct etiquette in India. With forty years on and off in the country, he could teach me how to manoeuvre more gracefully within a country of great need.

Our boy from the Shiva temple ate all the food and snacks, poised and almost elegant, a true gentleman. An array of thoughts swirled through my mind as tears came washing down my face, watching his grace. How often I have complained about the most inconsequential things. The vast energy I could waste on things I thought I wanted, or what I thought I lacked. How I could be so self-centred and egotistical, even in my search for my most spiritual self.

The flood of emotions was not only mine. The entire group around us became emotional. The boy exuded authentic, deep gratitude for the small food offerings we had given him. Kids I know in western countries have every gadget and gizmo available, iPads, iPods, iPhones, fast computers and video games. Yet they moan about not getting that present that all the other kids are getting. They lack perspective to consider giving to another, or how much harder things can be for others.

I would send them all to this little boy from the Shiva temple. Such huge gratitude in such a small body, with no parents or teachers in sight demanding that he be thankful. This young teacher led me to a realisation of how discontentment is so widespread in this digital age. We care more about how we look to others on social media, instead of caring for the *feelings* of others, or taking time to be of *service* to others, expecting nothing in return.

He was our little Guru, teaching through his shining example of surrender, courage, kindness, divine refuge. I saw a great soul, not measured by material possessions, but possessing a well of wisdom deep within. I pray I never forget this boy, my teacher of truth and gratitude. His memory still inspires perspective in me, to this day. Humility and trust in the little boy of the Shiva temple.

Vraj pilgrimage

I TURNED 23 ON MY first birthday celebrated in India, and the greatest gift was showered upon me.

Kalindi Bahuji led a Vraj *Yatra* pilgrimage that year, in memory of her departed husband. She was a woman Guru leader, and with the help of Shyamdas, my God brother Vallabhdas and I requested to join the *Yatra* pilgrimage. I had heard about this *Yatra* from other devotees and was excited, though I knew little about it, other than it was to last forty days, and we were to walk barefoot, while singing love poetry of the Vraj area.

"I give this to you for your birthday gift." Kalindi Bahuji said in her broken English, beaming, her dark brown eyes reaching straight to my heart. I had been given the greatest blessing and gift of my life, the pilgrimage of a lifetime.

A middle-aged woman with an air of grace about her, Kalindi Bahuji carried an aura of love and acceptance. She was often surrounded by doting devotees, and it was hard to get physically close to her, though a peaceful presence surrounded her from the moment I met her.

Thousands of pilgrims took part in the *Yatra*, from all parts of India, from all classes of society. Camps with tents were set up for pilgrims so that each day, at the end of ten to twelve hours of walking in the footsteps of great leaders, teachers, and pilgrims through the sacred sands of Vraj, we arrived at our assigned camp, laid out the same in each site so that we had familiarity with our camp home.

Each morning, I bathed in a bucket of cold water in a makeshift canvas tent with an open-air roof. We all bathed with clothes on so as not to expose our naked body, quite a trick on some confused mornings. But I preferred this daily austerity, foregoing the warm buckets available to earlier risers – I needed my few extra minutes of snoozing.

This cold water helped to wake me – we started to walk each morning at around 5am. After my bath, I joined my fellow pilgrims, where they drank chai tea and shared *nasta snacks.* There were eight pilgrims in our tent, elderly Gujurati ladies from retired business families. We sat on our cots sipping tea. As early rising was not my strong suit, I could barely think straight, let alone eat, though I knew throughout the day we would have plenty of opportunities to nibble.

The loudspeakers placed around the encampment broadcasted the route of the day. Moments later, the arrival of the Guru in the main area was announced, and she led pilgrims out for the day's walk.

Walking amidst thousands of people every day was an extraordinary feeling, accompanied as we were by the sound of our group chanting and singing. It was as if we moved together in synchronicity to the inner beat of the group, heart rhythm in unison as we made each step with ease, floating amidst the sacred chants and love poetry. We were like gentle feathers gliding down a river of voices, soft sweet sounds caressing the air with our breath.

"Mangala Mangalam Vraja Bhuvi Managalam"

Blissful auspicious world of Vraj, world of auspiciousness.

When I first heard the beginning of this famous poem written by Shri Gusainji (Shri Vallabhacharya's son), I heard the English word "booming" in there: it made me think of the profound transformative 'booming' effect that living on the Vraj *Yatra* had upon us. Booming with greatness. Booming with enlightened people. Booming with spiritual energy. Mundane problems and the dramas of everyday life dripped away, and we were beckoned into our true original nature, pure bliss. Though the actual word is "*Bhuvi*" meaning "place in the world," my kirtan was:

"Mangala mangalam Vraj is booming Mangalam"

A devotee from Dwarka walking next to me one day, sang a beautiful chant. A small woman, she seemed like a child at first, until I noticed sweet age on her face – just barely, as women in India have beautiful skin and hair that do not give up their age. I listened to her melodic chant, and tried to join in. She paused from time to time to correct my words in such a gentle way, then continued singing with such joy!

"Jai Yamuna Shri Govardhan Nath

Mahaprabhu Shri Vitthal Nath

Shri Vallabh Vitthal Giridhari

Shri Yamuna ji ki bali hari"

Hours flew by without a thought, as we were both absorbed in chanting and walking.

Before we knew it, we had arrived at one of the first holy sites of that day. A Shri Vallabhacharya *betak ji*[52].

It was the season of Holi, the festival of spring and colours. Men and women of all ages ran around the holy temples like children, throwing coloured powders at each other and smearing each other's

52 a place where Shri Vallabhacharya sat to teach 500 years ago.

faces. I soon found myself covered from head to toe in delightful shades of red and purple.

My new friend from Dwarka surprised me by creeping up behind me and smearing red kum kum powder in my hair and face. She burst into child-like laughter at her surprise attack on me. I spit the red powder from my mouth, and laughed back, blinking red powder from my lashes. It was a shocking and amazing experience. Adults, often so sombre, are given time off at Holi from all their seriousness, and play with pure, prankish, joyous fun!

That evening back at camp even my cold bucket bath wouldn't wash away the colours that were sinking into my skin. I was still breathing red, and my mouth was even tasting red red red with the coloured powder. When it seemed that cleansing the colour from my hair and skin was going to be impossible, I gave up and resigned myself to the fact that I had now become a more colourful person!

Barsana is the birthplace of Shri Radha Rani, the most beloved female counterpart of Shri Krishna. I was sitting alone under a tree near the main tents of the camp, when suddenly dark clouds slid into the golden sky. It had not rained during the entire pilgrimage, and the rumbling thunder and lightning were a surprise. The lightning seemed to illuminate the entire sky, outlining the shapes and colours of the dramatic clouds.

Golden eagle-like streaks, red and orange ravishing rainbows, along with the many deep, beautiful sea-blue shades, as if the ocean had flipped above us, waves and all. I had not seen a storm so beautiful. Lightning tore through the heavens with the speed of a cheetah, thunder growling in its path. Within just a few minutes the sky again cleared, and a calm golden-light haze remained where the sun was setting, the storm still hanging on in the east. It seemed as if the heavens had opened, and divine chariots would soon come forth from within this mystical haze.

Then, it rained. I lost track of anything around me, rapt by this *darshan*. Heavy rain pelted the earth, washing away some of my rainbow colours. The rain lasted only a moment, and left me drenched, seeking shelter under a tree. I had experienced a Radha Krishna Holi play right there, in the stage of the sky. I sat under the tree to meditate and recite a prayer that I was learning called 'Gopi Gita' the song of the Gopi's.

> *"Jayati te 'dhikaṁ janmanā vrajaḥ śrayata indirā śaśvad atra hi dayita dṛśyatāṁ dikṣu tāvakās tvayi dhṛtāsavas tvāṁ vicinvate"*
>
> *"Your birth in the land of Vraj has made it exceedingly glorious, and thus Indira Shri Laxmi, the goddess of fortune, always resides here. It is only for you that we are staying alive. We are searching everywhere for you, so show yourself to us now."*
>
> *- Gopi Gita, Shrimad Bhagavatam*

> *"The Gopi's are the dairy maids of Vraj, simple cowherd women. They are the banners of love for Shri Krishna. They are the devotional stars of Shri Krishna Lila, written about in the famous Shrimad Bhagavatam. Shri Vallabhacharya Mahaprabhuji calls the Gopi's the highest Guru's of love for God on the path of Grace. They mastered dedication of their minds and hearts to Shri Krishna. Their total dedication is not merely a meditation, it is an active process, intertwined with inner and outward reality."*
>
> *–Inner Goddess -translation by Shyamdas*

Choti Maharaj

Not far from the Neem Karoli Baba's ashram in Vrindavan, lived Choti Maharaj, whose name means *small king*. To his thousands of devotees, he was known as Hanuman Das Maharaj. He was said to be over 125 years old when I met him. The oldest man I had ever met. He lived in a small ashram on the *parikrama marg* of Vrindavan.

His ashram was on one side of a narrow, dusty road, and just across the road was his small cow farm. He lived with other sadhu monks, simple village folk. He was full of *Krishna Bhav.* His devotion was to his Bala Krishna *svaroop* and serving the cows and pilgrims. He was pure love incarnate. Anyone who was fortunate enough to receive his pat on their head, knew the bright shining love that radiated out of his body through his wrinkled hands. He served hot chai tea with milk from the worshipped cows from across the path, sometimes with delicious *prasad.*

He was said to have left his home in Kumaon in the foothills of the Himalayan mountains when he was just 10 years old and became a *sadhu.* He was a dear friend of Neem Karoli Baba Maharaji, and shared magic stories about the famous Guru, pulling out tattered photos of himself with Maharaji in their younger days.

With just a smile he filled us with joy each time we made those cherished visits; his room was warm and safe; his mood was of loving kindness. Incense wafted through the room and the soft patterned mat we sat on was worn from the many pilgrims who had visited, paying homage to this small king saint. Sitting quiet as a mouse in the presence of such a delightful and grace-filled soul, listening to his soft voice, I didn't always understand the words, yet feelings of profound love energy swirled in my chest and all around me. I bathed in pure love.

He was slow of speech yet full of strength. Compassion sparkled from his eyes like twilight stars. We would sit in *satsang,* sometimes talking, sometimes singing and chanting *kirtan* and *mantra.* Or sometimes sitting in silence. It could look like nothing at all was happening; no grand explanation of life or the discovery of deep meaning, just pure good association, free of anger, judgement, jealousy, or greed.

Then came the pat. He patted each of us on the head as we left to return to Neem Karoli Baba's ashram for the evening. Each time we visited, tears welled up inside, a lump in my throat, and I tried to hold back the flood that wanted to burst through. It was such an intense emotional experience. I had not been the crying type, during childhood I trained myself not to cry in fear of Father. Here in this ashram of the small king, a space that felt like heaven on Earth at that moment, a love-filled abode – tears or no tears I was accepted by his pure love.

The pat of his warm gentle hand tapping on top of my head sent rivers of golden light into my body through the top of my head. The touch of pure love coursed through my vulnerable body and straight into my fragile heart. Divine grace was in and all around me, healing from within.

One day Vallabhdas and I visited the small king saint and found him out with the cows across the road. This was one of the first times that we saw him in the light of day, our usual visits happening at dusk. We saw him in a better light, a very small skinny man, with dreadlocks longer than his tiny body. He usually piled the dreadlocks into a nest on top of his head, but it was impressive to see the dreadlocks snaking to the ground, every bit as long as he was tall.

One of his Sadhu monk helpers informed him that we had come to visit, and he slowly made his way over the muddy cow farm and across the road to us, as he leaned on his devotee smiling saying

'Radhe Radhe'.

We sat in his room in the ashram for some time, in silence. Then he spoke.

"Sing some *kirtan*." He smiled at us.

He asked one of his devotees to pull the harmonium from under his bed and motioned us to play and sing. I was very embarrassed, new to playing the harmonium and did not feel qualified to sing for this great saint. I was anxious and inadequate, not sure what to do. My cheeks flushed a burning red. As if he knew our hearts, he smiled and started to sing a beautiful Vrindavan *Kirtan*.

"Radha Kundo Krishna Kundo, Giri Govardhan, Madhura madhura bansi baje yahai Vrindavan."

With his lead, he motioned to us to join in with the blissful *kirtan* chanting experience. The embarrassment that gripped me moments earlier seemed to have disappeared, replaced with a mood of true love and acceptance. Over and over we sang to the rhythm of the Vrindavan melody he was chanting. I choked up every time for the love and kindness we experienced there. His *kirtan* over, he looked at us and smiled. Again, he asked us to sing.

This time I was ready to play, no judgement, no fear, no expectation: time to surrender to openly sharing with this love-filled saint. I played the harmonium and sang another Vrindavan favourite. The small king joined in, happy and joyous like a child. I opened my eyes and saw the small king crying. A river of tears flowed down his childlike face. Tears of pure love and joy. Melting my wounded heart.

After the chanting, we sat in a blissful silence. A deep meditation absorbed us in the ashram room of the small king. Only the sound of the breath could be heard, we were again bathing and breathing in love. After some time, the small king saint said with a gentleness:

'Prem – love'.

He smiled, creasing his deep dark deer-like eyes, held up one finger and said,

"Eki prem." Only love.

Home of Choti Maharaj

Walking into your heavenly abode
Simple small and sweet
Every time overflowed with deep emotion
Crying at your lotus feet
In your presence a love never experienced before
Heart opening wider than the sky
Tears streaming down to the soft floor
To cleanse and purify the true me
Each word each hand each foot each time more
Infinite love, infinite light

Oh beloved, how to express the love you gave that made us soar
Such fathomless beauty and grace
I once knew a true saint

- Vrindavan 2006

The gateway to God

In Nathdwara, Rajasthan, a town with significant Pushtimarg history, I was fortunate to spend time deepening my relationship to sacred music. Some say this town and the surrounding temples is the main gateway and centre of Pushtimarg, this is where many devotees come to serve and sing and be in satsang together.

I arrived there shortly after completion of my 40-day Vraj *Yatra* pilgrimage. I spent days full of busy *darshan* at the three main temple Havelis, time sitting with lineage holders of the path of grace, all of which were masterful musicians or beautiful wise mysterious men and women. Evenings were spent listening to the sacred music as they played ancient Pushti Haveli Sangeet-style music, mesmerising and melodious.

Hearing this music straight from the celestial choirs, I was transported. I became entranced, blissed, as we stumbled home to our guesthouse after these late-night sacred music evenings. In those days my deep devotion to classical Indian music began, and every day we participated in *Pakhavaj*[53] and singing lessons of Pushti Haveli sangeet style *Kirtan*.

Teaching methods in India were different from anything I had experienced. We practised one single drum beat over and over again. And over again. And over. Though I couldn't hear what we

53 ancient indian drum.

were doing *wrong* to deserve the punishment of such repetition – it felt like writing *"I will not…"* 100 times on the blackboard in school. To be honest, I was feeling impatient. I wanted to learn a full drum sequence and was growing bored at practising just a few sounds in each lesson.

Just when I was about to give up, our drum teacher played a full sequence of the drum language, and I was rapt. His hands moved so quickly, vibrating so fast that our eyes could not catch more than a blur. Perfection. Meticulous movement. I couldn't see where his hand was touching the drum, but the sound that emerged was heavenly. He played with such absorption, and I realised that we were in the presence of a Master drummer, and I would bow to however he wished to teach us.

I surrendered and became disciplined in my *abhyas* practice. I repeated our homework over and over again. And over again. And over. Luckily my roommate was also studying the drum, and the two of us encouraged each other, both of us obsessive and inspired daily.

In the afternoons we took singing lessons. This teacher, who we called Mishraji, was like a grandpa, welcoming and warm. Lessons were on a top terrace, and we climbed very narrow stairs to his music room, arriving out of breath, where we would start class with a warm chai tea.

Mishraji impersonated each of us in a comic way – he joked and made us laugh till our tummies hurt. He looked at me and pretended to flip hair over his shoulder and say something silly. He had a way to zero in on everyone's essence, just by studying them for a few moments. I often thought that laughing was the perfect warm-up exercise, getting us to move and breathe in the diaphragm.

Wise Mishraji came from a lineage of temple singers, going back hundreds of years. He sang devotional love poetry for God each morning in the local temple, giving him freedom in the afternoons to teach us. Once chai, laughing and chit chat was over, it was time to begin our lessons. Mishraji would play a melodious tune on his harmonium, then he would begin the traditional, classical warm up called *Alaap. Alaap* is like scales, moving through the sounds of each note within the *raga* Indian melody.

After warm-ups, we sang Pushti Haveli *sangeet*-style *Kirtan* love poems. Mishraji paused from time to time to present his amusing English translations of the love poem. With a cheeky grin, he would say

"Do you understand? Yes OK , OK again."

A sparkling grin and a twinkle in his eye and we continued, off into the love realms of Krishna and Radha through sacred music. The hours of class with Mishraji flew by.

A feeling of ancient power swept over me in these lessons, hearing Mishraji play and sing. I was transported to a timeless place. With gentle ease he encouraged us to join and moved to a solo for each of us in the *raga* that he was teaching. Nerves overtook me when it came to my turn, my cheeks burning red, I was afraid to get it wrong or sound completely off. It was much easier when we were singing together. When it was solo time, my vulnerability was at the surface, and I could hardly breathe.

"It is good, come on, we want to hear from you." He smiled with encouragement.

"Louder, sing louder." He cried with joy and smiles which softened my nerves slightly.

I closed my eyes and began to sing louder. I felt my confidence grow as I kept singing while Mishraji was playing the harmonium and giving me reassuring smiles. I let go of the mind stuff and surrendered to the moment with these dear souls, breaking through my shyness and nerves, I was free to sing.

"OK, more tomorrow, OK. Yes?"

And suddenly class was over. Too soon for me, I wished it wouldn't end. I nearly floated back to our guest house, the *raga* resounding inside of me, the love poem filling my mind and heart. His charming, friendly nature helped me over the months and years to find my voice and have confidence sharing and singing.

I wrote this poem with a divine friend when I was deeply inspired by my time living in Nathdwara; the people, the worship, the love for God. I was enchanted by the people and experiences – a genuine love and acceptance I had never felt before. One day through blissful tears, this poem came rushing out of me onto paper. A glimpse into the heart of devotion.

This divine love

Always waiting, yet totally absorbed
Burning turmoil, yet wonderous feelings
You fall in love, yet rise
The more you drown in it, the more you survive

This divine love

Uncertain, yet perfectly clear
You keep giving all you can, yet it satisfies your own soul
Robbed of all, yet the richest
In everything beautiful, in every breath

This divine love

It gives you pain, but you always want more
It fills you to your soul, yet you remain thirsty
Heart wrenching separation, yet sweet union
Out of place, yet truly belonging

This divine love

Destroyed, yet whole and complete
Afraid, yet fearless
Lost, yet found
It makes you a great speaker, yet renders you speechless

This divine love

Overwhelmed, yet peaceful
Carried away, yet firmly placed
Nowhere to run, yet constantly chasing
Sometimes unreasonable, yet the reason to live

This divine love

Never on time, yet perfectly timed
You would do anything, yet can do nothing
Smooth, yet crooked
Absolute truth, yet upside down

This divine love

One, yet infinity
Mesmerised, yet fully awakened
Unbelievable, yet the only belief
Indescribable, yet described by his dear ones

This divine love

Hidden, yet shining bright
Heart aches, but never breaks
Solid as a tree, yet soft like butter
Free, yet bound

This divine love

Hopeless, yet the greatest hope
Remembering, yet forgetting
On top of the world, yet under a mountain
In times of struggle, the only shelter

The only place to turn, in every instance, in every moment

This divine love

- India 2006

My life had been changing with great speed, as my spiritual experiences in India deepened. Everything about the path of grace had enraptured my mind and heart. I was so overwhelmed with gratitude that my heart was aching with love. This famous *grace* song came flooding in caressing my still very wounded traumatised heart.

> *"Amazing grace, how sweet the sound, that saved a wretch like me. I once was lost but now I´m found. Was blind, so blind but now I see."* I was singing my heart out.

Return to the West

Nat: Parataro mantro
Nat: paratar: svatah:
Nat: paratar: Vidhya Tirtham
Nat: parat param

"There is no mantra, prayer, knowledge or holy place more superior than the blessed state of inner continual loving mood."

- Nirodha Lakshana
-Shri Vallabhacharya Mahaprabhuji

VALLABHDAS AND I ARRIVED AT JFK international airport in New York, returning from India after my first six months there. We wore traditional Indian dress, with various markings of *Gopi Chandan*[54] and red *kum kum powder* smeared across our foreheads. In the mood of devotion and love, the ancient love poems we had learned resounded through our minds and hearts, memories of India still dancing within us.

We approached the customs line. I was travelling on my New Zealand passport and hoping for a visa on arrival stamp that most New Zealanders get and that I had already received countless times

54 Yellow powdered sacred sand.

before. I was eager to fly through customs back to my American home. At this point in my life, I had travelled in and out of the US for many years. Coming and going, going and coming. With happiness and genuine respect, I greeted the stern customs officer, and he answered me with a look of great disdain, asking me many questions.

"What is the purpose of your visit?"

"Who are you staying with?"

"How long will you be here?"

Suddenly, I was whisked off to the side and sent into an interrogation room.

I knew what was going to happen. This had happened to me earlier on a trip through London. Border agents seem trained to question people who look like me, a little different, a little exotic perhaps. They think that we are coming to work illegally and overstay your visa allowance. They asked me many questions, mostly around money. I was honest and spoke from my heart. I told them that God takes care of me, that I always have enough.

When asked if I had ever worked for money in the US, I told them no, which was true. I never worked just for money. I do what I love for my passion to help others connect to their mind, body and soul through ancient practices. This is my work and my life purpose, which I do not do for money. Money does, of course, flow my way. The border agents were not impressed, though I caught a couple of them smiling.

They decided not to deport me but I was not given entrance. I was to obtain a visa in New Zealand. It was not so bad, time for me to return to paradise.

The customs officer explained in a very American accent:

"Today, Madame, unfortunately we will not be allowing you entrance into the United States of America. However, if you go home to your country and get a visa, you'll be able to come back in no time."

Through the glass window, I waved "Goodbye" to my companion, Vallabhdas, who had been patiently waiting a few hours at the exit, hoping for a miracle. Two immigration officers escorted me to the terminal where they arranged my flight back to New Zealand. Along the way the officers talked to me, friendly and curious. They asked me about India, why I liked it so much. I told them about Yoga practices and how anyone can do Yoga, even them.

"If you can breathe then you can do Yoga."

I taught them a few simple *Pranayama* breathing techniques and we did them together while waiting for my flight. They had to remain with me, to assure that I would not "escape." For hours we enjoyed interesting conversations about God, the universe, Yoga principles and day-to-day life in India. I brought India with me and shared it there in the JFK airport. Even though I wasn't to enter the US, it mattered to me that I could share these experiences, hoping to uplift someone's life in some way. Even immigration officials.

My India

Home again eternal space
Nothing but his divine grace
Seems like I never went away
Unbounded timeless day
Don't want to close my eyes
Lovers know that is not wise
To miss a moment in his playground
No other place that I have found
Delightful sounds enter the ears
Now letting go of all fears
Feeling sacred sands caress my feet
Our bodies bristle with joyous heat
Tasting sweet nectar inside
For eternity may I reside
In my beloved's supreme place
Where I find his shining face
-Vrajdevi

Life back in New Zealand was strange. I was so absorbed in my new-found Yoga lifestyle in India that I became a foreigner in this place that I had called my home for so many years. My parents did not understand what I was doing early every morning, chanting and practising Yoga.

I missed the smell of dried burning cow dung in the narrow streets of Vrindavan, the screeching car horns and the playful pilgrims singing *Radhe Radh*e with abandon. Life back in West Auckland was plain, rigid, and colourless. My parents were still in a very dark hole since the loss of my sister. It had barely been two years since her passing.

I tried doing Yoga and breathing exercises with them. My father got fed up with a few minutes and didn't want to follow my instructions. My mother, however, diligently followed every instruction and I could feel the pain trapped deep in her mind, body and soul. Often through a veil of her tears I rubbed her back, transmitting healing energy. She sighed with momentary release from the pain that was killing her inside.

In India it is often said that your parents are your first Gurus. I used to scoff at the idea. My parents were the *opposite* of any Guru I had met in India. However, I did feel a great sense of duty, especially towards Mother. I wanted to share with her some of the healing love energy that I had been experiencing in India. As difficult as it was to spend time around Father, I put up with him so that I could be of service to Mother.

I would dress her in the traditional women's' *saree,* wrapping seven metres of cloth around her. I put bangles and jewels on her. Shy and modest, Mother never really dressed up, and this was like playtime for her, bringing a small smile to her otherwise heavily drawn face. I would make us traditional Indian chai tea and vegetarian dhal soup with special fried rice. She enjoyed as much as she would allow herself.

I stayed with my parents for a couple of weeks before I was again ready to move on. My sisters then lived in Australia, so sometimes

I stayed with them. I worked teaching Yoga and giving healing massage treatments in New Zealand, Australia, or the US for six months to make enough money to travel back and live in India for six months. India's maximum tourist visa lasted only six months, so for many years I continued living half my year in India and half in the West.

When I was away from India, I missed her every single day. My heart was in India while my physical body roamed through Western countries. India was and still is my home. Its people and places stole my heart. Some people I meet who have been to India focus on how much they did not like it. India is the abode of contradictions, and depending on your company there, everything can change. I was so fortunate to be with some of the most inspirational lovers of God. My experience, though often challenging, taught me lessons that were refining and defining me.

It was during my roaming in the Western world, in between regular trips to India, that I had the opportunity to visit Ram Dass in his home on the island of Maui. I was enchanted by this Hawaiian home, his temple shrine room adorned with a glowing picture of Maharaji. We sat together with his friends and aides to chant and pray. The love emanating from this space was like a huge warm shower of light. His smile was calming and ever-present, exuding gratitude.

One morning as I took my usual walk in the garden, I spotted Ram Dass sitting alone in his kitchen just off the garden – an unusual encounter, as he was always surrounded by devotees. I did not want to intrude on his cherished alone time and turned to creep away back down the garden path.

Ram Dass called out,

"Ram Ram." The holy name of God recited as a greeting.

I could not ignore him, so I turned around and greeted him. Feeling shy and awkward, I said that I did not want to disturb him, but he smiled and motioned for me to sit with him.

With no idea what to say, I smiled as my cheeks blushed red.

Smiling back, he asked "Is there something I can help you with?"

He had read my mind and heart. I was feeling at that time caught with two minds about a decision I needed to make, and it needed to be made that morning. Reluctantly I related my dilemma.

"What do you want?" he asked.

"I don´t know, I have no idea."

"Yes, you do know, what do you want?" He asked me again, insisting and louder in his tone.

No one had ever asked me that before in my life, at least no one who really expected a straight answer. My decision was so difficult, as I was afraid, I wouldn't choose what I really wanted, afraid that what I really wanted would end up letting people down, people I loved and cared about.

Again, his voice boomed at me.

"What do you want? Tell me. You know what you want." His beautiful blue eyes seemed to look straight through me. I could not hide.

I was struck speechless, afraid to speak my truth. I tried my best to control the thumping in my chest. The lump in my throat was growing. I knew I must respond. When I finally mustered the courage to speak, it was between tears, but I felt that a huge weight was lifting with each word. Too eager to please others, I had never before asked myself with complete honesty what *I really wanted.*

I knew I could not lie to Ram Dass, he was staring at me square in my eyes, non-judgemental, compassionate in his mystic blue eyes. Reading my heart, I knew only the truth was possible today – a truth I had been avoiding for fear of hurting my Paradas family back in the Hamptons.

I had found such comfort there, with the secret garden, the warmth of their family, having cared for the children for years, bonding with Lalita and Ramesh. They were the family I never had, the family I dreamed of. Yet a part of me knew it was time to break with this comfort to focus on my mission in life outside of them. It felt impossible to leave the safety, love, and protection of this family.

What Ram Dass pushed me to admit that morning would become an important empowerment tool: I had permission to truly listen to my inner voice. My true voice had been too often buried by the fear and oppression of my New Zealand home life growing up. What I wanted hadn't been important.

Now was the time I would begin to believe in myself. I was ready to step out of this comfort zone and really start on my journey of independence, sharing the gifts I had been given, and connecting to my own valid space, my self-worth.

With a heavy heart I told Ramesh and his family that I would not be accompanying them back to the USA. I needed to stay longer in Maui and have some time for myself to decide what was next. I moved into a cottage not so far from Ram Dass´s home. It was a place called Shanti gardens. It was there I met more devotees who inspired me to chant Kirtan with them every day. It was magical and enlightening. My path of Bhakti was stronger than ever.

> *"Our whole spiritual transformation brings us to the point where we realise that in our own being we are enough."*
>
> *– Ram Dass*

The so-called terrorist

I HAD ARRIVED BACK HOME again in Vrindavan, India, and received an anxious call from my mother in New Zealand. Armed police, a full swat team, had raided our family home just a few days after I had left. They confiscated some of my things after turning the house upside down. They even rifled through my sister Iraena's bedroom, which my mother had kept just as Iraena had left it only three years before. It was a massive intrusion for my parents, the behaviour of the police that day was threatening and aggressive. We were not new to this authoritarian attitude from New Zealand police, but the incident was shocking. They even had a police helicopter circling our home from above.

My parents were shaken, recalling how the police had failed to help my sister the night she went missing. Now they were accusing another daughter me, of being a terrorist, looking for incriminating evidence which was simply not there. They even had a warrant for my arrest. My mother knew that I had done nothing wrong; we had no idea why the police were there. It had to be a weird mix up.

News started to come out of people being arrested, people I knew personally. The narrative spun at the time was that these people were suspected of terrorist activity. I recalled with a sinking feeling; a day spent in my tribal homelands a few months before.

I have both past- and current-day Māori rebels in my family; interesting characters who keep true to their staunch tribal ways.

One family member I'll call "The Green Warrior." *Green*, as he is covered in *Ta moko* from head to toe. His skin carries a rainforest hue from the tattoo ink covering his skin. *Warrior* because he comes from Tuhoe, our tribe which has been world renowned as home to some of the most-fierce ancient- and current-day warriors.

I ran into him one day at a friend's radio station where he was a regular host. Instantly we became good friends. Somehow, he knew my family ancestral background without me telling him too much about myself. He liked me and we had deep conversations about life and joked easily. He used to laugh and say that he wondered why the fancy radio station even asked him to host radio shows.

"Perhaps because I'm notorious in New Zealand now, a staunch Māori activist."

He invited me to visit our tribal lands with him. I jumped at the opportunity and within days I was off with a few friends on a road trip, singing love songs and greatest hits for the three-and-half-hour car journey. Young and old gathered on the tribal lands for a few exciting days, learning to read the forest and practising some warrior training, focusing on activities to help better channel angry youth.

Undetected and trespassing on private tribal lands, police and investigators planted undercover cameras, with the intent of demonstrating that our Tuhoe lands were terrorist training camps. They recorded our adventurous time together and had been doing so for a number of months. Turns out they followed a number of people in this group, suspecting us of organising a terrorist training camp, of all things. I personally was uninterested in these outdoor activities and running around the forest. I just wanted to continue spiritual conversations with the Māori elders.

The whole idea of a terrorist training camp was ludicrous, because terrorism was not a thing in New Zealand. It felt so invented to even talk about terrorists. Charges were eventually dropped, and the police came to the tribal lands years later to formally apologise. The accusation was absurd from the start but mimicked with great similarity the incidents of our Tuhoe past.

Once again tribal members were persecuted for no good reason, or because they were influential in their community and did not follow oppressive fear-based ways – echoing the story of another influential man from my tribal lands, not that long ago, who suffered adversity at the hands of the Government of New Zealand at the time.

The story is set in the tribal lands of Te Urewera in the Bay of Plenty, a place my father never took us as children, a place he would have rather forgotten. A place I discovered when I was 19 years old, a heaven on Earth. Unbounded natural beauty, untouched by the outside world.

Rua Kenana – Leader, Spiritual Healer and Peaceful Activist

Rua Kenana was a prophet and healer from the tribal lands of Te Urewera. Rua stated that he was the successor to *Te Kooti*[55], after having had a deep spiritual experience upon a mountain called Maungapohatu, the sacred mountain of my tribe, Ngai Tuhoe.

The oral narratives tell us how Rua and his first wife, Pinepine Te Rika, were directed to climb the mountain by a supernatural apparition, later revealed to be the archangel Gabriel. They were shown a diamond, the hidden guardian-stone of the land, whose bright white light was protected by Te Kooti's shawl. Rua, in his turn, again covered the light to protect the secret. Rua met both Whaitiri, the ancestress of Tuhoe, and Christ on the mountain. Rua would soon claim to be the Māori brother of Jesus Christ.

In 1907 Rua formed a non-violent religious community at Maunga Pōhatu in Te Urewera. The community, also known as New Jerusalem, included a farming cooperative, a savings bank with a growing community of over a thousand people. Many colonial British labelled Māori as 'lazy and drunken' so the return of self-respect and independence under Rua Kenana irritated them.

55 Te Kooti Arikirangi te Turuki- A Māori leader.

In a meeting with the prime minister at the time, Sir Joseph Ward, in March 1908, Rua accepted Ward's argument that there could be no separate Māori government.

'There cannot be two suns shining in the sky at the one time.›

Rua also interpreted this to mean that the same laws would hold for Māori and Pakeha alike, because they all enjoyed the same one sun that shone above their heads.

Rua's leadership was based on the principles of equality and peaceful non-violence. Even so, he was seen as a threat to the New Zealand government. Authorities saw Rua Kenana as a disruptive influence and targeted him with the Tohunga Māori Healer Suppression Act 1907. It banned traditional Māori healers from using their herbs and other traditional healing methods. The Tohunga Suppression Act was designed to neutralise powerful traditional Māori leaders and acted as a de-facto political weapon against Rua Kenana and his expanding community.

The plan of the colonial government was to diminish the dignity and heritage of the Māori people. During World War I, Rua and his people were continually harassed by the police. Rua insisted that his people boycott military service, arguing it was immoral to fight for an English king and country, given the injustices Māori people suffered under British crown rule in New Zealand at the time. This was just what the government needed, ammunition and an excuse to go after him.

A first attempt to arrest Rua in February 1915 was unsuccessful and a year later in March 1916, seventy heavily armed police were sent into their peaceful community in Te Urewera at Maunga Pōhatu mountain, with orders to take him and his community down. He was arrested on April 2nd 1916 after a shootout between his followers and the police. Rua's son was shot dead. None of the invented charges against Rua stuck, though he was found guilty of a lesser offence – moral resistance.

The trial held in the Auckland High Court lasted 47 days and was the longest trial in New Zealand history at the time. The judge sentenced Rua to 12 months hard labour and 18 months of imprisonment, a very heavy sentence for the minor offence of moral resistance. Eight members of the jury signed a petition protesting against the harsh treatment of Rua Kenana.

After serving nine months in Mt. Eden Prison in Auckland, Rua returned to his followers in 1918. He was in bad health due to mistreatment while in prison and weighed down with legal costs from the trials that had built up over years. The prison staff and the prosecutors had a change of heart for this weary old man. Obviously, he was no threat to anyone. Rua was given safe passage back to his peaceful Maunga Pōhatu community after his shortened imprisonment to find his people broken and divided.

While many people had already left his peaceful settlement, others stayed with him until his death in 1937. Rua Kenana was a leader, spiritual teacher, healer and peaceful activist, beloved by the people. But in the end the Colonials stopped at nothing to break him and his people who were trying their very best to live in harmony and freedom. His efforts were directed toward gathering people and inspiring them to live and work together in a beautiful and revolutionary way.

This episode was just part of the drive by the government to break down Māori communities. False accusations and misconduct came from a system that was charged with creating law and order. My father was born just a few years after the passing of Rua Kenana. The years of true peaceful warriors were over, and violence, abuse and neglect reigned supreme in many homes – including mine.

For the past 170 years Tuhoe people have been dealing with misconduct by the police. Rua Kenana's story mirrors what happened in 2007 to the Green Warrior and my tribal people. The police and armed forces were waiting to pounce on the most outspoken modern activist of the time. Though the majority of charges were later dropped, the police and the New Zealand government flexed their muscle with impunity and were not held accountable for their misdeeds.

Police raided my family home in Auckland. They raided the main village of my tribal lands and other locations simultaneously. Dressed in raid gear and heavily armed, they stormed the tribal lands turning everyone into suspects. They even stopped a children's school bus and pointed guns at children who were made to lie face down on the ground. Unbelievable behaviour by the police force yet again.

Before I was to return to New Zealand from India, my mother informed the police of my arrival, with her simple innocence she asked them not to come to the airport on that day, and that she would be sure that I would report to them once I was home. I arrived at Auckland airport and my mother was relieved to see me, with no police and no handcuffs present just yet.

A few days after settling home again, while I was cooking, doing my morning prayers and offerings, there was a loud knock on the front door. Sudden shouting. I climbed a few flights of stairs to the front door and saw two police detectives through the side glass panels. I opened the door and greeted them.

"Good morning gentlemen, what is the matter here?" I asked with a smile.

I was dressed in my traditional Indian *saree* with mantra music playing in the background.

"You are coming with us." The detective insisted.

"What do you mean? What have I done?"

"You know exactly what is going on Miss, don't play stupid."

"Oh yes that's right," remembering mother had already informed them about my arrival back in New Zealand. "My mother told me you'd want to talk to me. Would you like to come in for some chai tea for a chat?"

I smiled through my annoyance.

"No, you will be coming down to the station with us." The officer snarled.

"Are you arresting me right now?" I enquired further.

I was more curious than anxious, doubting that these police would take it that far and arrest me, a Yogi. I had never been arrested in my life and dedicated to peace, love and truth. Arrested? My heart began to race.

"No, there's no warrant yet. But we can get one. Would you like that? Do you want to be arrested?"

He was getting frustrated and infuriated now.

"And what would you arrest me for?"

I was shocked at his fury-filled response.

"If you come with us now, we can avoid all that." He was losing his patience.

"I am a bit confused, so you are not arresting me, yet I must come with you right now. Is that right?" I tried to make sense of the nonsense.

"Yes, exactly. That is exactly what I am saying."

He was adamant now, inching towards me, hungry on a power trip.

"OK, but first I must change into something a little more appropriate for the police station. I think this *saree* I am wearing is a bit bright."

I laughed pointing at my bright pink and purple flowing *saree* gown. I hoped the detectives would lighten up a little. But they did not.

"We'll wait inside then." He seemed to think I would try to escape.

"No, I don't think so. It is best you both stay out here. I am only going inside to get dressed. I'll be back in a few minutes. I am not going anywhere. There is only rainforest behind the house. So, no escape route there." I laughed again trying to lighten the mood yet again.

"Don't do anything stupid, or we will arrest you," he warned as I closed the front door.

Confused and annoyed, I went to my temple room and finished up a couple of things before I changed into other clothes. In those few minutes I saw through the windows in my sister's bedroom that one of the detectives was trying to scale the side of my house. The detectives were becoming more impatient, knocking again at the door. I quickened my pace, ate some fruit offerings, then opened the door again to the edgy officers.

"OK, I am ready."

I smiled on the outside, as a tool to keep myself calm. On the inside I was annoyed because I knew I had done nothing wrong, and they were treating me like a criminal. I learnt in India over the years, to be accommodating and accept any wrongdoings on my part. I had done no wrong and knew that they were amid some sort of delusion. I knew everything would work out. The truth always prevails.

Rolling their eyes, we headed out and I went to my car.

"Where do you think you are going?" The officer was angry now. Getting close to me as if he was going to grab me. I carefully moved backwards.

"We're going to the police station, right? I will follow you. I know where it is. I can meet you there, I have my own car." I pointed at the green Toyota in the driveway.

"NO! Enough of this! You must come with us!"

"Look, I don't know how long we are going to be, but I would prefer to have my own car with me. So, if you don't mind I can just follow you, if that makes you feel better."

I grinned while gritting my teeth, I would not back down, and I was not going in their police vehicle.

This all became absurdly humorous, two grown men acting like such brats. The angry officer spoke with his partner, and they reluctantly agreed to follow me.

In the police station, as if from a movie, they locked me in a room with mirrored windows for the "interrogation." I knew they were watching from the other side. After some time, they came into the room with folders, and asked me why I thought I was there.

"Because you knocked on my front door this morning and said I was required to come here."

I smiled again. I reminded myself to breathe deeply, as the air had become thick with the dark energy of judgement. The energy swirling was heavy with anger staining the walls of this little room.

They showed me pictures, some of them of my extended family. They wanted me to identify who I knew, but I had nothing to hide. Yes, I know the people in the pictures and yes, I hang out with them. Was that a crime? Is it illegal to have activist friends and family?

Then they showed me a picture of me, in the tribal lands one of the days of the alleged "terrorist training camps." In the picture, I was wearing my favourite boots and Prada sunglasses, recently missing from my home.

"Oh yes!I have been looking everywhere at home for those boots and glasses!" I then realised they had probably taken them as evidence.

"So that is you in the picture, at the training camps. You are admitting it." He lurked uneasily over me.

"Yes, that is me. I have nothing to hide. Do you have these boots and sunglasses that belong to me? When will I get those back?"

After I identified myself in the photo, they proceeded to formally arrest me. I told them I would not speak to them any further without a lawyer present. Annoyed, they locked me into a holding cell, perhaps to scare me. But this small dark room gave me an opportunity to do my Yoga practice interrupted that morning. Now and then the prison guard opened the slot on the top of the door to check on me. I'm sure he had never seen anyone doing a Yoga practice in the cell and chanting Sanskrit *stotras.*

Thanks to many years of Yoga and chanting I was at ease knowing that God would take care of me. We like to think we are in control, but in my years in India I learnt how the only thing I can really control is my mind. In this cell I surrendered, momentarily. A little voice inside of me shrieked,

"Oh my God! You are in big trouble! You could go to jail!" I allowed the voice to express that fear, then shifted my perception to the bigger picture, to God's love and protection.

> *"Elevate yourself through the power of the mind, and do not degrade yourself. The mind can be your best friend and your worst enemy."*
>
> *- Bhagavat Gita Chapter 6, verse 5*

This verse was resounding inside my head, and I was allowing my greatest friends to be present in my mind: God, love, truth. I was at ease, sort of.

I finished my Yoga practice and began meditation. As hours passed, I began to feel a kind of caged energy. Trapped in here for no good reason, they were trying to take away my freedom. Instead of sitting in sadness and fear, I meditated. I chanted a very special Sanskrit mantra, which takes fifteen minutes to complete. If I was to be physically trapped, at least my mind and heart would soar free.

I lost count of how many cycles I completed, so immersed in this deep meditation. I meditated on compassion for others incarcerated, and for the guards. I recalled great leaders such as Nelson Mandela and Mahatma Gandhi, who were also falsely imprisoned, and yet they shone bright like stars and continued as true leaders, true inspirations. The pain and suffering we experience in one moment, can be transformed in the blink of an eye, going inwards, toward our own inner wisdom.

I remained in the cell for most of the day, until the guards opened the door in the evening and the same detectives whisked me up some stairs.

"So how did you like that? Not such a glamorous place. Imagine staying much longer inside a place like that. You would not want to find out how terrible a place like that can be." The investigator probed me.

"You do know all of this can go away, if you help us and tell us what we need to know."

Again, as in movies, the bad cop pushed me to cough up information to save my own skin. I had no incriminating information, nor did I know what exactly he wanted me to say. Even if I had information, his behaviour from that day inspired no trust.

"Tell us about Tame Iti, '' he insisted, using the Green Warrior's given name.

He is your uncle or something right? Why should you be punished for things that he has done? Your life could be ruined because of such a terrible man." His seedy agenda was evident.

Tame Iti was a kind man. He was family and with this smear disrespecting an elder in my tribe, the investigator crossed a line. I brought to bear other lessons from India: tuning into the right things in conversation and tuning out of the negative aspects. I chose to tune out as they led me along corridors of the police station and into a police car.

"I am going to give you a chance to tell me anything, before we take you down to the court where we are formalising the charges against you." He tried and failed once more.

"I have nothing to say until my lawyer is present, thank you." I was tired now and really wanted to go home. I had no interest in playing their pathetic game.

After going through the formal procedures in the court, I was allowed to go home. As I was leaving, the investigator snarled a few last comments and handed me his card if I changed my mind and wanted his help. I was so pleased to leave and drive home. Tired, drained, but grateful that my spiritual practices and the grace of God had kept me safe.

Nothing ever came of charges against me, the system had failed again wasting time, money and energy in all the wrong places. Justice and truth will always prevail. If this whole debacle had taught me any life lesson, it was for certain the realisation that corruption and misconduct can come in any guise. Uniform or no uniform, failure to follow decent human respect was no path for me.

Mother my first Guru

When my mother was fading away from this life, I was far away on the other side of the world. Sad and confused, I ignored the ever-more-evident fact that my mother was a mere mortal. I never entertained thoughts of losing her, except when I was a know-it-all teenager amid teen angst, hormones running high.

All that far behind, I was shocked and now trapped in disbelief, losing any thread of hope that my mother would rise from her sick hospital bed. Only a few days before, I talked to her and she seemed like her normal self. Now she was in a coma and my sister had me on video call from London to Auckland. I was singing healing chants to her for over an hour as my sister held the phone to my mother's ear. Holding back my tears and gulping for breath, my heart was pierced in pain.

I've known friends who have lost mothers. We all lose our mothers at some point, but until death came to my own mother's door, I couldn't imagine the absolute helplessness and pain, the sleepless nights, that truth haunting each breath.

God has a plan; I believe this with all my being. Death is not the end, but a transformation from one body into another form. While this is all good and well as an abstract belief, the truth is, I was not ready to lose my mother, the immortal one, the strong woman who had been through so much her whole life.

She had just retired, when the brain tumour attacked in full force. The doctors called it a very aggressive tumour. In my foolish hope, and suspicion of the 'western medical world,' I believed that this tumour was but a remnant of past suffering she had endured. She would certainly overcome this and recover. After all, she had been through much worse. Little did I know as I tried desperately to sleep at night, the tumour had already taken over. The angels had summoned her, and within 48 hours, she was gone.

Mother had waited 15 long years to reunite with my sister Iraena Rama Te Awhina, The Light Helper, and now she would remain in her eternal embrace, so desperately desired.

My mother gave birth to four children. Later, when I became a mother myself, I would understand the selflessness, the sleepless nights, the giving, always giving – and the forgiving. As a teen I was headstrong, not conscious of the stress my sisters and I caused our mother. And she forgave us all in a heartbeat. Forgiveness is one of the most difficult lessons we learn, and I had a strong example in my mother.

The day of the funeral, I landed in Auckland International Airport, with only an hour to spare before the funeral service. I had to race through the airport, and then race by car to my home. But first I had to clear customs.

"Have you got any food? Have you got any honey? Are you sure you don't have any apples?"

I was so nervous about time. The interrogation went on and on and on.

"No, no, and no!" I was furious.

"I have nothing, nothing at all! What I have is my mother's funeral in an hour!"

Stunned, the customs officer ushered us through. I was a wreck. I had travelled over 30 hours to get to New Zealand and was fully exhausted on every level. Despite the ridiculous apple interrogation, I was going to have time with my mother before her body left our family home, for the very last time. Come what may, I would arrive on time.

I arrived at the appointed hour, jumped out of the car and raced past the many family and friends gathered. I stepped into the house, and my mom was in her bedroom. All the furniture had been taken out except for the coffin where she lay. My two sisters were next to her. I embraced them and broke down.

It hit. I wailed and cried and shook in shock at the sight of my mother lying dead. I sat scrunched on the floor with my sisters, looking at them, looking at her – searching for a way to process. I was suddenly drawn to the sound of the clock ticking. I needed to pull myself together for a special ritual and prayer for my mother before she was taken away. My sister asked everyone to leave.

The three of us remained with our mother. I touched her dead body with sacred sands from India as is my custom. I cried, shaking. This was the first time I had touched a dead body, so cold, hard and stiff, all life force drained. Wrenching as it was, I tried to bring the prayers forth without completely breaking down. Placing my right hand on my mother's chest, I held hands with my sisters. A powerful rush of energy ran through my right hand and into my body, to my heart. The waterfall of reassuring golden light encompassed us. A moment of peace settled upon us, and I could feel my mother's presence, her soul.

I opened my eyes and told my sisters that I could hear Mum saying,

'Oh, you silly girls, so much crying?'

We all burst into laughter, a moment of lightness in the darkest of times. The darkness returned quickly, and our smiles returned to tears. The funeral crew had arrived. In a flash the room filled with strangers. They were preparing to take her. My moments with mother were done.

I said goodbye to this body of my mother, the one who knew me from the beginning of my life inside her womb. My heart ached and pain consumed me. I was drained, dizzy, hopeless. The lid of the coffin was placed over her. I would not see her body again. One of the funeral crew handed me a bolt to seal up the coffin. I trembled as I went through the motions. They lifted her coffin out of the room and to their hearse.

'Your mother is your first Guru.'

When I first went to India, I heard that phrase often from my spiritual teachers. I didn't attach any real meaning to it. My mother as my Guru? No, not mine. She probably taught me what *not* to do in life, but I hadn't recognised her teachings. With time, the phrase bloomed for me. Mothers give birth to us in this world. Mothers sacrifice, know everything about their children, tolerate all our stormy moods. And despite all, mothers are always present for their children, with a heart full of forgiveness and love.

The Gurus recognized mothers as teachers. Teaching to love and to be loved, to forgive oneself and others. To accept and not expect.

This is a poem that flowed out of me through my tears. In honour of my mother, as we flew in the plane across many oceans and continents to return to my homeland of New Zealand and face the loss of my mother.

Dedication to my Mother

Selfless service is what you did best
You tolerated all types of juvenile unrest
Being ever so ready
Not always so steady

Hand on my heart
It is time that we part

I never thought this day would come
When all would be dusted and done

Thank you for being my mum
May your light shine bright like the sun
Into God's embrace
A flowing river of grace

We will think of you my dear
No place for any fear
May your spirit soar free
Into eternal life you will be

Ashes to ashes

At Te Piha, the infamous west coast beach in Auckland where my sister had passed 15 years earlier, we gathered to spread my mother's ashes, as she wished. The day began with a soft misty rain, grey clouds lingering. I thought back to the mist of that other day in Te Piha, when the gentle touch of the mist maiden *Hinepukohurangi* softened the edges of our mourning and kept us safe in her blanket.

We were going to dive into the icy cold rugged west coast waters to immerse our mother's ashes. Holding fragile flowers in our hands, we were not looking forward to taking our clothes off for the full immersion into the raging Pacific. Father handed me Mother's box of ashes to carry down to the water's edge.

I had never imagined my mother would end up in this box. Not the spirit of course – I know she existed now free in her natural soul state, but these physical remnants, now in ashes in this box. We will all end up like this. Ashes to ashes dust to dust. However, in this moment the reality for every one of us became hard and clear: death of the physical body, inevitable, no one escapes. My own physical mortality weighed down on me like tonnes of bricks, heavy on my heart.

We listened to the prayers of Matua, a Māori elder, a relative. He had come that day to deliver the final prayers for Mother. When it was time for my father to speak, in his shaking, unsteady manner, he tried to apologise to Mother for not being the best of husbands.

There was a slight glimmer of humility and guilt in his trembling voice. The terror he had put her through, the pain he was carrying – we could feel the heavy cloud of guilt and shame weighing him down into the cold wet sand.

Then it was time for the daughters to immerse her ashes and say our final prayers. With heavy and aching hearts, we went through the motions to prepare, gulping tears. We changed into our bathing suits, ready to do our one last service in honour of our mother.

With purpose we strode down to the water's edge. We felt Iraena's presence with us that day. Four of us accompanied our mother to her final space on this earth. As we approached the water, the clouds parted ceremoniously, and the sun beamed through with great intensity, illuminating the spot where we stood. The rain ceased and sunlight funnelled in, as if the love of God and all our angels came shining through straight to us, compassion, and love in a shower of light.

My sisters and I smiled at each other, amazed. We would not fail her final wishes. Mother shined her blessings upon us. We sang our hearts out to our mother's favourite Elvis Presley song *'Can't help falling in love with you.'*

> *"Wise men say only fools rush in. Well, I can't help falling in love with you. Shall I stay? Would it be a sin? If I can't help falling in love with you? Like a river flows surely to the sea, darling so it goes some things are meant to be. Take my hand, take my whole life too. For I can't help falling in love with you"*

As we scattered her ashes into the sea, we were tossed by waves and currents. The sea was tame in comparison to some of the treacherous days that we had experienced at Te Piha. It seemed that even the ocean helped us in our endeavour that day. Scattering the ashes, I was saddened by these final rites for our mother. My sadness was tempered by a sense of peace, knowing that at last my mother was now reunited with her beloved daughter, taken from us far too soon.

The waters would allow safe passage for the spirit of Mother to be free once again. Dancing with the dolphins back to the safe shore of God's love.

> *"E rere, wairua e rere" fly spirit fly...*

We emerged from the sea and wrapped towels around our icy bodies. The final ceremony was done, Mother had gone home to her true spiritual home, her long awaited peace to fly free. Our lives now changed forever.

My earthly sisters and I were to spend the rest of the day at a women's retreat centre, just minutes away from the beach. We arrived at the centre and instantly a warm home vibe filled us.

The elderly woman who managed the retreat was kind and wise, the embodiment of women's empowerment. She summoned us to take nice hot showers and treated us to a lovely vegan meal. The sun beamed, and the day bloomed into a beautiful blue-sky sunny day. We had found a safe place to heal after a day of many emotions.

After a lifetime with Mother, of trials and tribulations, after all she had done to shape four beautiful, kind girls, it was time for my sisters and me to heal more deeply than ever before. I was grateful to be with my sisters and other kind, compassionate women. The day we dreaded had transformed to a bittersweet memory, etched in our hearts.

> *"Lord, make me an instrument of your peace:*
> *where there is hatred, let me sow love.*
> *where there is injury, pardon.*
> *where there is doubt, faith.*

where there is despair, hope.
where there is darkness, light.
where there is sadness, joy.
O divine Master, grant that I may not so much seek
to be consoled as to console,
to be understood as to understand,
to be loved as to love.
For it is in giving that we receive,
it is in pardoning that we are pardoned,
it is in dying that we are born to eternal life"

Saint Francis of Assis

The days and months following Mother´s departure were filled with memories and processing of the life she lived. The time we had spent with her, the challenges she faced, and how much suffering I saw her experience. As I was reflecting with my sister one day, I experienced a deep realisation as if Mother was giving us a message, to no longer mourn her life and struggles, but rather to recognize that we as her daughters have an amazing opportunity: she was not able to live an empowered warrior woman's life, yet we were given life through her and we could live our lives with more purpose, more love, and more empowerment. It was an inspired moment of revelation.

We have the opportunity to love instead of fear, to live with joy instead of sadness, to breathe blessings instead of anguish. To be kind instead of cruel. We didn't have to carry the pain and suffering she had endured. While she was alive, she wished the best for us. Now that she entered a different realm, her instructions for us to carry on were loud and clear.

"Live your life with joy and love, live happy and free, you have so many gifts and you should share them with the world.

> *You are empowered warrior women. Live fearlessly and serve others through this wisdom of the empowered woman."*

Since my sister disappeared all those years ago, I had dedicated my life to Yoga and other ancient healing practices, and to the union of mind-body-spirit that Iraena had so desired. Still traumatised and healing myself, I would shy away from bigger opportunities for fear of failure and my *not good enough* story. Yet just before Mother passed, I had begun serious one-to-one women's wellness sessions in Spain where I currently reside.

Using a combination of these ancient healing modalities and working with women who have suffered a variety of mind, body, emotional and spirit trauma, I still questioned myself and my capabilities. With my mother's message in my heart, the time had come, perfect or not perfect. Fully healed or not fully healed. There is only *now,* and life is short. Years ago, when I had the vision of my sister in my dream in pure bright radiant light, I made a promise to God, Bhagavan, to the supreme universal power energy, whatever you wish to call it.

> *"Dear Lord, I will try my utmost every day, to surrender to your will. To accept all the good and bad that is given to me and to devote my life to helping others reconnect to their mind-body-soul purpose. I know you are with me, please make me your instrument. Let me remember your love and light through all my darkest times."*

I was ready more than I have ever been, to share, sing and shine the light of love and healing on others. My *not good enough* story has faded into the background and my mission and soul purpose now stands in the forefront of every day. There is nothing else I would rather be doing. As an instrument in service to others, to encourage and inspire other women on their journey is my greatest honour.

Finding forgiveness for my failed father was one of the hardest things I've done. However, in time I can see this tortured man who never truly learned to love or be loved. Forgiveness is not accepting the bad behaviour and allowing it to continue. Forgiveness is the release in the heart, releasing any malice towards any being. To set my own heart free I have forgiven him.

The worst moments of my life still stand to this day, those events around the loss of my sister Iraena Rama Te Awhina. Yet the way my life transformed from that trauma into a mission of women's empowerment has left me trusting without a doubt the divine beloved plan behind all the waves of love and life.

Reflections 2022

IT HAD BEEN NEARLY THREE years since I was home in Aotearoa New Zealand. Called back to attend to family matters, I was deeply emotional after the long absence of the Covid years, and I experienced incredible healings and shifts while there.

Unexpectedly, my sisters and I received a special gift: part of the jawbone from the whale that had beached itself after our sister's disappearance. As is traditional, all those years ago, a part of the whale jawbone was bestowed to a Māori elder of that area. During my visit, he shared part of this bone with my sisters and me. Honoured to receive this valuable totem, we asked a whale bone Master carver to work on carving *Taonga*[56] for each sister and one for our father.

My family blessed these Taonga in New Zealand in the sacred river of my tribal lands after I left for India. My sister Lainie brought the whale bone Taonga to me there, where we blessed it in the sacred river of my local area in Vraj. I felt the bone pulsating with powerful energy: a full cycle of healing had taken place. This whale had sacrificed itself, and though we would never get my sister's body back, we now hold a great treasure, a piece of this whale.

In New Zealand, the healing which took place between my sisters and me was a great gift from God. We healed deeper than ever before. We have united stronger than ever. The past traumas that

56 Taonga: A precious gift.

have gripped at us for most of our lives seem to have dissolved; love remaining the only law that binds us together.

India is a great spiritual home for me. I was fortunate to step foot upon the lands again after many years away. My heart was full of awe, honour and reverence in the weeks I spent there. Many of my teachers had passed on, yet they remain closer to me than ever before. Divine souls, dear friends, remain embodied, dedicating their lives to devotion and service, inspiring and filling my heart with joy.

The simplicity of village life, the humble hearts that see only spirit.

You do not need a big ashram or big group of people following you to be a great teacher.

Sometimes it is the hidden unassuming woman that sings outside the temple that is the greatest teacher of all.

Spiritual revolution is now, we are the ones we have been waiting for and we are more than ready. Ready to love more, serve more, dance and sing more, live more. This is the time to unite and dive into the revelation of who you truly are.

Thank you
Namaste
Vrajdevi

Endnotes

Hinepukohurangi - Goddess of the mist, sacred feminine
One of the ancient stories of our tribe is about how the children of the mist came to be. The story begins many thousands of years ago. Maunga Pōhatu (sacred masculine) was a star being of heavenly realms who was drawn down to Earth by Hinepukohurangi's charm and beauty. He became a comet and landed in the tribal lands to meet with Hinepukohurangi. Their divine explosive love union created Potiki.

Then from him came the tribe, Nga Potiki. The original people of my tribal lands of Ngai Tuhoe - The human star-like people. The children of the mist. Balanced integrated beings, peaceful and at one with the land. They were in tune and could communicate on many levels with the natural world and the divine. The song lines of mauri flowing through all of existence.

'Mauri ora mea katoa'

Hinepukohurangi, her mist places delicate touches throughout the land. She is integral to the very life breath of the land and people, her shape ever-changing, mysterious. She is spellbinding. She is the Goddess of the mist and lives among her descendents eternally.

Shri Vallabhacharya Mahaprabhuji, 1479 – 1531 – Founder of Pushti marg (Path of Grace)

Shri Vallabh was a child prodigy, by the age of seven he had studied the four main Vedas. He acquired mastery over the main Indian philosophical systems. He studied Shankara, Ramanuja, Madhava, Nimbarka, Buddhist and Jain philosophies. At the tender age of eleven he was present at a debate where all the top scholars had gathered in Krishnadevaraya Maharaj's court. He was given a chance to speak, and he won the debate. On that occasion he was honoured by being given the title 'Acharya' (Great Teacher) and 'Jagad Guru' (Teacher of the world).

He made barefoot pilgrimages around India three times in his lifetime of 51 years. Most of his life was dedicated to explaining and elaborating on the foundational Bhakti texts, making commentaries on Shrimad Bhagavatam and Bhagavad Gita. He has revealed in his writings that without the Lord's grace, it is not possible to know the inner meaning of the scriptures or Krishna's *lila*. This is what he taught to his disciples in these various *betak ji's*. Twenty-two of his teaching spots are to be found in the Vraj area, and 84 *betak ji*'s are spread throughout all of India from the time of his original pilgrimages.

According to the teachings of Shri Vallabhacharya Mahaprabhu, there are four different devotional moods that can be cherished towards Shri Krishna. The devotee can be the Lord's servant, friend, parent or lover. The devotional attitude of being the *'dasa'* or servant is the foundation of Pushti Bhakti marg. While the relationship of being his friend, parent, or lover, occurs with the Lord's grace, the manifestation of grace cannot be limited.

Ram Dass 1931 -2019 - American spiritual teacher

Ram Dass, formerly known as Richard Alpert, was a Harvard university professor in the 60s. It is there that he teamed up with Timothy Leary, and together they experimented with psychedelic drugs on humans.

This began a spiritual journey and awakening, deepening when he met his Guru, the famous saint Neem Karoli Baba in India. Ram Dass wrote many books, but the most famous and fascinating book is *Be Here Now.* Ram Dass later went on to give lectures across the globe. He established many charity foundations and gave his inspirational wisdom and teachings freely.

He brought the Yoga of Love to the West through the empowerments he received from his Guru Neem Karoli Baba. He still has a huge impact on the spiritual seekers of the world. I recommend all of his books and lectures.

Please visit https://www.ramdass.org/ for more incredible teachings of this bright soul Ram Dass.

Bhakti

Bhakti is said to be the foundation of all Yoga. The solid tree is Bhakti and the branches of the tree are the various forms of Yoga for example, Meditation, Karma Yoga, Wisdom/knowledge of Yoga etc. It is the natural and easy way of being in our true original state. There are many practices of love and service connected to Bhakti, yet it is said that Bhakti on a certain level is every breath you take, as it is taught by the great Bhakta Prahalad Maharaj in the Shrimad Bhagavatam. There is a nine-fold path to follow in the way of Bhakti.

Shravanam - Learning to listen deeply to others and oneself
Kirtanam - Praising through song and story
Smaranam - Remembrance of your divine connection
Pada Sevanam - Service and honour to the feet, humility
Archanam - Worship and honour to the divine
Vandanam - Respectful honour
Dasyam - Becoming a servant of God and others
Sakhyam - Becoming a true friend to God and others
Atma Nivedanam - Soul dedication

Suradas, 16th century Devotional poet and musician

Suradas was said to be born around 1478. He was born blind and neglected by his poor family. He left home when he was a small boy and although he was blind, he had incredible inner wisdom and psychic insight. It did not take long before people who met him started gaining from his special power of association. Soon a larger number of people gathered to worship him as their Guru.

Knowing his fame was spreading, he left all his followers to seek refuge in God alone. He had already been composing poetry and songs in honour of Lord Krishna. One day as wandered India, he happened to come upon Shri Vallabhacharya in Gokul. That is when Suradas´s world changed, and he renounced all his followers to become a follower of Shri Vallabhacharya.

Suradas was one of the main Kirtan singers and poets of the Pushtimarg lineage. He composed thousands of devotional love poetry songs in honour of Radha and Krishna. His poems are still sung to this day in temples and homes across India. His heart which lives through these poems was a great contribution to the Bhakti movement around India and the world.

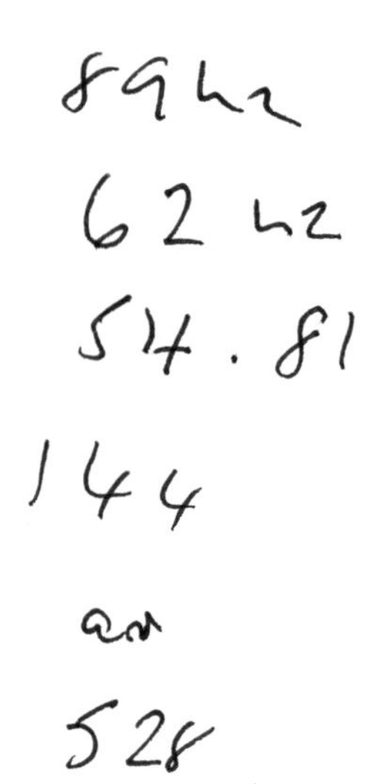

Printed by Amazon Italia Logistica S.r.l.
Torrazza Piemonte (TO), Italy